Second Nature Leadership

FREDDY CACERES

First Edition

PAGE PUBLISHING, INC.
Conneaut Lake, PA

First originally published by Page Publishing 2020

ISBN 978-1-6624-1266-0 (pbk)
ISBN 978-1-6624-1267-7 (digital)

Printed in the United States of America

This book is dedicated to a wonderful, loving, and supporting woman, my super wife, Lina, for her endless love and inspiration and my great parents, Juan and Nieves Caceres, for paving the way to my success.

sec·ond na·ture

noun; a characteristic or habit in someone that appears to be instinctive because that person has behaved in a particular way so often

Contents

Preface

There are several stages of leadership and countless definitions to the word. In order to be an effective leader, many factors must be taken into consideration. There have been several thousands of books on leadership in addition to the countless hours of seminars delivered by seasoned presenters sharing their leadership knowledge and experiences. The influx of leadership information available has allowed millions of readers and seminar attendees to sharpen their leadership knowledge and learn the traits of those that have delivered the information.

Contrary to the statement "knowledge is power," I have suggested a change to that popular statement to "applying is power." We as leaders or aspiring leaders can have all the knowledge in the world on how to be an effective leader, but if the information is not constantly applied in the workplace, then we only possess leadership knowledge. This book explains many leadership traits and tactics that may or may not already be known to students of the game but may be new to less experienced learners of leadership. What is most important and contained in the pages to come is over two decades of management and leadership experiences and ways to apply experienced leadership traits. The continuous application of leadership qualities is the key to transform them into second nature traits.

There are several factors to effective leadership and a variety of leadership styles instructed by many authors and lecturers, and if simply a handful or two of those important traits are consistently performed, it will positively transform the way groups perform. But be certain that leaders are lifelong learners, and newly learned leadership qualities should continuously be added to your leadership portfolio. Once a new leadership quality is learned, it needs to then be put into action and applied. There is a big difference between absorbing information and putting what you have learned into practice. The Dalai Lama said, "It is necessary to combine knowledge born from study with sincere practice in our daily lives. These two must go together."

On several occasions, I have been asked if leaders are born or made. The answer is clearly that they are absolutely made. With changing times and generation gaps, leadership is an ever evolving trait that, just like tools, needs to be constantly sharpened. To be a great leader, one must have the unadulterated passion to improve, constantly crave knowledge, and adjust habits to successfully lead. The only way, and I stress *only* way, to stay sharp and effective is to constantly learn and apply the traits used and taught by effective leaders. When the traits expressed in this book are consistently performed and put into action, you will soon do them almost without thinking, and in turn become a second nature leader.

Acknowledgments

This book has been long in the making and has been developed through experiences in over two decades of management and leadership experience. Many of my supervisors, coworkers, and subordinates have had much to do with my motivation to go through with completing this book, but no one has been more influential than my wife, Lina. Lina possesses some of the most natural leadership qualities that I have ever witnessed, and she has always supported me with everything that I have ever done.

A special thank you is also in order to my mother, Nieves Caceres, for giving me a great parenting foundation that I have passed on to my children and even employees in the workplace. Furthermore, thank you to my father, Juan Caceres, for pioneering my leadership development and always pushing me to be the best at everything I do. Lastly, I would like to thank my children, Ethan, Wesley, Ryan, and Abigail, for teaching me that leadership is a lifelong journey.

Introduction

It goes without say that growing up, we learn a lot from our parents, though we may not realize it until later in life. In many instances, we learn from our parents as well as through life experiences on how to be and how not to be professionally and personally. The same is such with current and former bosses on what to use and what to leave out of what we exhibit to our subordinates. We all possess a particular style of dealing with people but should make sure to adopt our positive and effective life experiences and incorporate them into our style. I have made sure to pick up favorable qualities from previous supervisors and made sure to leave out the ineffective ones that I didn't favor. In other words, and as stated by Woodrow Wilson, "I not only use all brains that I have but all that I can borrow."

I remember my father to always be a hard worker that put work first and everything else followed. I only knew him to have two jobs my entire life, but he somehow seemed to know a little about everything. At seventeen years old, I was as other kids my age, lost and wondering what to do with my life. At the time, my father was the operations manager for a telecommunications company named KM Contracting Inc., and he thought it would be a good idea to have me work for the company while I scuffled to figure out this thing called life. Thanks to my father's decision to bring me into the profession, my professional journey commenced, and it began to blossom to the point that I started to figure out more than just life. I began to witness the importance of organizational leadership and what works well and not so well when leading a team of employees toward an organizational goal.

As an employee for the telecommunications company, I performed to the best of my ability, and soon my hard work was noticed by the owner of the company, and I was asked to fill a vacant supervisor position. Eventually, I worked my way up the corporate ladder, and after nearly thirteen years of supervising employees, I was able to add to my internal human hard drive several methods that worked and pitfalls that proved ineffective when leading a team within an organization. I categorize this period of my leadership development stage as my sensorimotor stage, which is the childhood development stage from birth to around two years old. During this stage in my management career, I was only still discovering how employees were reacting to my style of overseeing their production and, well, non-production in some cases. I say overseeing because at this point in my life, I did not yet consider myself a leader but rather an employee that held the title of manager.

At this point in the leadership development stage of my life, I also discovered that the years will fly by fast when you're focused on the successful operation of an organization. The experiences learned at the company were very valuable to say the least, and as the years past, despite a fairly generous compensation for what I did, I was not truly happy with the job. I would later hear someone say that if you love what you do, you will never work a day in your life. Well, I must have really been working my butt off because I did not love what I was doing at that telecommunications company following in the old man's footsteps.

I soon came to the conclusion that if I wanted to be truly happy going to work, a place where we spend over one third of our lives, I would need to seek a new career path. That's when I decided that I would begin to peruse my dream of becoming a police officer. This career path would later enhance my knowledge and application of leadership qualities from what was already discovered at the telecommunications company.

Traditionally, a career in law enforcement begins in one's early twenties, but after so many years in corporate America, I was already years past the traditional age of a rookie cop. I was thirty years old and my son, Wesley, was recently born, so I knew the journey to begin a new career would be more difficult than a kid still living at home with mommy and daddy. I quickly realized that it was not easy to show up to the police academy before sunrise for physical training when you've been up most of the night with a crying newborn and when you were much older than most spring chickens running in formation alongside me yelling cadence at the crack of dawn.

But after successfully completing the police academy and happily commencing my new career as a police officer, I now got to sit back and see the sergeants do their thing. Quite honestly, after being in management for so many years, it was nice to be on the other side of the table. The easy part was that I always kept in mind what I expected from my employees when I was a supervisor, so this new position was a piece of cake. All I had to do now was what was expected of me and exceed my sergeant's expectations and enjoy a long prosperous career.

Not exactly. See, when you grew up working for a father like mine, you were programmed to shine and be the best at everything you do. My days at the rank of officer only lasted for a couple of years before I was promoted to the rank of sergeant. Here I was, only a couple of years in and already supervising seasoned fifteen- and twenty-year veterans. That took a special tactic in itself that I learned many lessons from. Eventually, I would rise through the ranks again and continue to add to my leadership hard drive the tools of the trade to create a workplace where employees possessed a positive vision of the organization and enjoyed being a valuable member of the team.

The task was challenging, considering that there was a negatively toxic culture in place that needed chipping away to restructure. I remembered the phrase "Rome was not built in one day" and knew that it would take some time and effort along with a true aspiration to make positive changes within the organization. I took on the task, and in doing so, I continued to learn what was effective and what was not while leading, which I will be sharing with you in this book.

Throughout the process, I did learn that not all leadership actions are effective actions. I discovered that some actions that came second nature to me were not always effective. A true leader will attempt to identify ineffective leadership habits and make the alterations necessary to successfully lead. Habits are actions that are triggered automatically but are not always effective in a leadership position. Interestingly, research has found that habit can be altered, and in doing so, the changes can lead to remarkable results.

Chapter One

First in, Last Out

Your actions define your leadership success. I guess Dad had a plan for me the whole time. As a seventeen-year-old, newly employed at a well-established telecommunications company, I first began to learn the ins and outs of what the job entailed. I also now had an opportunity to see my father in action as the boss at work rather than only his outstanding parenting skills at home. Dad possessed a unique mixture of management and leadership qualities. Already at this point in my leadership journey, I began to identify what may work for me if given the opportunity of filling a management position.

Dad was very firm at times, almost to the point of being unkind to his subordinates when needed. It appeared effective at the time because the job got done regardless of how the employees felt. The employees were unhappy at times, and occasionally, I would catch one roll their eyes at my father's ways, and more than once, I walked in on someone bad-mouthing Pops. So far, at this point in my teenage life, new to the workforce, I began to witness certain management styles that I would later in life realize were appropriate for the times. Those were the times of a different generation, and many things in work and life were more acceptable than they are today. It was a time of do-it-because-I-say-so-with-no-questions-asked. I will later discuss how adjusting your supervisor style to various generations is very important for a leader.

The owner of the company, Keith Manalio, appeared to love my father as the manager of his company. How could he not? Dad had not taken a vacation in several years and never missed a day of work. I used to remember my father bragging about being the one to disarm the burglar alarm in the morning and arming it at the end of the day and how he believed that the owner, Keith, may have forgotten the alarm code by now. His work ethics and loyalty successfully gained him a thirty-year career with the company. I would eventually work my way up to become a division operations manager for the organization and supervise over four hundred employees throughout my tenure with the company.

I somehow began to fill my father's very big shoes and put work before everything else. I always found it fascinating to arrive to work and see my father already there and at checkout time still there. He was always the first one in and the last one out, and for the life of me, I cannot remember my father ever calling out sick from work. These ethics were instilled in me at an early age and would later help benefit my professional career forever.

What was not taught to me was how to satisfy employees and not have them roll their eyes and negatively gossip about "the boss." The art of dealing with employees and creating a positive culture within an organization came from several years of overseeing employees and developing strategies on how to create job fulfillment and influencing a desire in them to also be the first in and last out. A desire to succeed and perform well may come naturally in some and may need to be developed in others. Regardless, a first in, last out mentality is sure to be beneficial at everything you do.

Vince Lombardi said it best. He said, "The man on top of a mountain didn't fall there." I titled this chapter "First in, Last Out" because it is what I witnessed my father do at work and also because it symbolizes hard work and dedication which needs to be witnessed by employees. To be seen as an influential leader is to be known as a loyal, hardworking employee even prior to your position as a leader. Excelling at your job can be contagious to coworkers, and when people follow your lead as a dedicated worker, you are already a leader within your group before you actually hold the official title.

When my career shifted from a telecommunications operations manager to a police officer, it was only a matter of short time before the promotion came because it was so easy to supersede my supervisor's expectations. Remember the quote "If you do what you love, you'll never work a day in your life?" Well, I was certainly loving what I was doing, so the answers to all requests by my supervisors was always yes. Stay later, come in early, or change my days off to fulfill the needs of the organization. "Yes!"

I did it because of witnessing professionally what my father did and also because I loved what I did. But oddly, there were many around me that were disgruntled and very much disliked the agency that we worked for. My mind reverted back to my management days at the telecommunications company, and I wondered how I could make a difference in the employees that did not share the same feeling as me for the job. It couldn't have been the job that we did because so much is involved in becoming a police officer that they had to be doing it for the love of the job. What was present at the time and evident was the cause-and-effect reaction of the ineffective leadership that was in place and lots of work needed to be done to positively transform the organization's members. A first-in-and-last-out employee like me knew that I would one day become an important factor in the transformation of naysay employees so that they, too, were as happy to come to work as I was.

No Alarm Clock Needed

I vividly remember being a kid and having a fun event scheduled for the next day, such as a field trip or a family trip to Disney World. The excitement in my mind had me awake before everyone ready for the trip with no alarm clock needed to wake me up. See, if you are doing what you really love and truly motivated with your job, you will be up bright and early, ready to take on the tasks of the day. For many years, I did not even need an alarm clock to wake me up in the morning. When I first began my law enforcement career, I was always excited to get to work, and at the end of a shift, I was not always ready to go home. I would listen to the police radio on my way home and hear calls being broadcasted on the police radio that I wished I was responding to. I was ready and eager to get back at work the next day, and I wasn't even home yet.

That feeling that I had early in my career must have somehow faded in those disgruntled employees. It was very hard to believe being that it was a never-a-dull-moment type of career. I later came to realize that it was not the job that had them feeling that way, rather the lack of motivation and support coming from the top. Yes, a job can get routine, and not everyone will always hold on to that exciting feeling of a new career. For that reason, it is the leader's responsibility to keep the workplace exciting and always create new ventures for the employees to embark in. Empowering employees to take charge of certain organizational missions will give a sense of ownership in the tasks and will inspire them to perform well at them.

As a patrol officer working at the same rank as my coworkers, I was always a hard worker and helped everyone out as much as possible. I demonstrated hard work and dedication and diverted negative talk by gradually changing the subject. What I was trying to do was to inject an antidote into an environment of dissatisfied employees and build comradery within the group. I would later become a sergeant and have some more leverage to motivate and influence.

In my position as a supervisor on several occasions when the organization was seeking change in a certain area, what we did was include the employees in the decisions and obtain their feedback on the issue. We reached out to them for suggestions and made them feel like part of the team rather than just implementing a change and advising them of the change after the supervisors had thrown it around to finalize it. In them, being a part of it gave them a sense of ownership in the task. Employees tend to support what they helped create and will work hard on it.

Going as far as entirely assigning a desired change to a group of employees and letting them run with it gives them a feeling of rights toward it and will get them out of their daily routine. It will also assist in the newly implemented change to get carried out more successfully because the employees were the ones that came up with it, hence trying harder to make it succeed. In doing this, though, we sometimes have to compromise with them and accept their decision for the change, even if we wouldn't have done it that way ourselves. Not an easy thing for some supervisors. Including the employees and caring about them was successfully seen in the outcome of Hawthorne effect, a study by Western Electric in the Hawthorne Factory in the late 1920s and early 1930s. The original reason for the study was to study the effects of the physical conditions at the workplace and its effect on productivity. The study included two groups, a study group and a control group.

The study group had the lighting and conditions in the work area improved, and the control group remained the same. The study group also had other things changed such as their work hours and rest breaks. The work productivity immediately improved in the study group, and the control group's remained the same. Ultimately, the lengthy study concluded that it was not actually the working conditions that increased productivity but the fact that someone cared about them and their work area. When leaders genuinely care about the employees, they will be more motivated to come to work and are less likely to need to be awaken by an alarm clock, and a first-in-last-out desire will become more probable.

I have heard that there are no secrets to success, only hard work. I would happen to agree with that statement. Greek philosopher Socrates said, "Let him that would move the world first move himself." Leadership requires hard work, and there is no way around it. My father was a hard worker that seemed to know how to do everything in the company. Hard work, dedication, and knowledge will definitely take you far in any organization.

A friend of mine who I respect dearly, Al Henderson, is a project manager for a well-established construction engineering company. He took me on a tour of the company's shop one Sunday morning as he had some personal business to take care of there. Al needed to stop by the shop to weld a couple of pieces of steel for a project he had going on at home, with the company's approval, of course. It was a rather large warehouse, and I remember seeing many large machines, not currently in use as the shop was closed, and we were the only one's there.

After a tour of the establishment, to my surprise, he asked me to do the welding. Well, I had never welded a day in my life and have to admit that it was pretty neat that he trusted in me to do it. After a short tutorial, I put on a welder's mask and got to work. I later thanked him for teaching me how to weld, and I remember him stating, "Always try to know a little more than the person standing next to you." The fact was that Al was not a welder for the company and actually did not perform many of the physical tasks at the company, rather a hardworking project manager with knowledge in every area performed.

Be a Student of the Game

Part of a first-in-last-out mentality should include the devotion to learn as much as you can about your business and run it with enthused dedication. One of the most valuable things I learned from my father was to be the hardest worker in the room. My father would definitely disagree with the quote "If you are the smartest person in the room, you are in the wrong room." Your business needs hardworking leadership for it to stay in shape. You need to be a student of the game in your profession and try to learn all aspects of it to become the smartest person in the room.

My oldest son, Ethan, wanted to join the Air Force to become a pararescueman (also known as a PJ). Prior to even enlisting, he joined a private training organization that trained young men and women that aspired to join the special forces in any of the military branches. Lucky for Ethan, the instructors were all ex-military Special Forces men and women that knew exactly how to prepare you for a challenging training regimen given by our great military.

Ethan came home one day after a strenuous day of training and told my wife and I that one of the instructors, an ex-PJ himself, asked him to name one fallen PJ that has died in combat. Unfortunately, he was unable to name one and detailed to us the earful that he received from the instructor. He said that the instructor added by saying that he would never recommend a recruit for the PJ training course that could not name at least one fallen PJ. I asked Ethan what he was going to do, and he said, "Nothing! What am I supposed to do?"

That story and his reply alike were like music to my ears. This was a great opportunity to guide Ethan a little closer toward a successful mentality. I told

Ethan to research five fallen PJs and learn everything about them and, the next time he sees the instructor, to respectfully approach him and ask to speak to him. I further told him to begin to name off the five fallen PJ's names and to give some brief information about each one of them. When Ethan came home a few days later, he described how he provided the information to the instructor, without even be asked to do so, and how impressed the instructor appeared to be. I get the feeling that the instructor may have recommended him for the PJ course.

Ethan was entering a profession that he knew little about. He was working very hard to prepare for the Special Forces training that he was soon to begin. The instructor was not only preparing Ethan physically but also mentally by teaching him that he had to be a student to the game in his profession. I'm pretty sure that what the instructor really wanted was for him to come back to him with the answer to his question. He never asked Ethan to research it, but I'm very sure he would have been asked the same question again at the next training session had Ethan not approached him with the information.

Having a knowledge of all aspects of the organization is important even if you are not the one that physically performs all the tasks. Most tasks are performed by employees, and it is important to know how to perform them yourself as you may need to step in and lend a hand, as I will later discuss further. Delegating tasks can be important, but pure delegation should never be an option, and a true leader must know when to pull her or his weight and lead from the front.

I remember during my time as a patrolman, I always made sure to keep in physical shape for the obvious reasons for a police officer and also to possess the command presence that every officer should have. In the later years when I worked my way up the ranks, I began to sit at a desk for much of the day, and my physique began to change. It surely didn't help that many executive lunches were included into my work week. What I noticed was how quickly one can physically get out of shape and how hard it was to get your body back in shape. The same is true for your business. If you do not properly tend to your organization, it will, too, get out of shape quickly and take long to get back into the shape it should be in.

Being a hard worker is key, but a leader should not be afraid of setting aside some of their work to allow time to spend with employees. A supervisor that leads by example and is seen as a hard worker is a good thing, but when care and attention is not given to employees, motivation and possibly production will diminish. Give employees a break from tasks and occasionally switch up daily norms to avoid stagnation. By doing this, they will realize that you care for their well-being.

When employees feel valued, they will in return perform well. In my police agency, there are various positions, such as public service aide, records department, dispatchers, and property room clerks, many of which aspire to become police officers one day. I express to them to act as if they are still on a job interview for the positions that they desire while working in the position that they currently hold. There are many that want to move into a different position, and there may be a short window to prove yourself to get to the level you want to be at. Dedicated workers already employed in the organization should be rewarded and placed in their desired position as a result of their hard work.

Great employees will not have an issue doing most of the work, and those employees need to be rewarded in any way possible. A leader should expect that rewarding an employee may result in other less productive employees calling it favoritism. When the employees calling favoritism are identified, this opportunity should be used to clearly address that hardworking employees get rewarded for their performance. Perhaps, they, too, should perform to the level of a first-in-last-out employee.

Chapter Two

Employees Are Awesome

Employees are awesome, and they need to know it. Richard Branson, the founder of the Virgin Group, said, "I truly believe that if you take care of your employees, they will take care of your business." We are quick to take care of customers but unfortunately sometimes forget to take care of the personnel that tend to them. I have heard people say that employees do not leave jobs, they leave bosses. I know that to be true because I have witnessed employees remain at their place of employment and turn down better-paying jobs because of the way the leaders of the organization made them feel. They felt cared about and as part of the team giving them a sense of responsibility and loyalty to the organization. It becomes difficult to leave a place where you are appreciated and treated as an extended part of the organizational family.

Many organizations seek to have an elaborate team but for many reasons fail to retain great employees. A supervisor can usually be to blame for many of the reasons employees don't stick around or do stay and provide mediocre performance. A great leader is able to balance the company's needs and the needs of employees. Lack of communication is probably the number one factor cited with employees and their supervisors. Simply having a meaningful conversation with an employee can be very impactful. and in the next chapter, I will discuss how I constantly "check the pulse" of employees.

I unfortunately witnessed a lack of much needed supervisor/employee interaction early in my career as a police officer. Later in my career at my police agency, a new police chief, Luis Diaz, was brought in who possessed the true qualities of a leader. His input as it pertained to the organization was always dedicated to the "end user." When an improvement or change was to be implemented, he always said, "What does the end user want?" It was fascinating to see a person in a position of power that cared about what the employees that actually performed the operative functions of the organization thought. In the end, leaders have to do what is best for the organization and also be mindful of the workforce personnel carrying out the tasks.

I remember one summer taking a family road trip to Kentucky for a vacation to enjoy the countryside and mountain region of our great country. Sometime during the fourteen-hour drive up from

South Florida, I saw a tractor and trailer in front of us traveling in the same direction with some lettering on the back of the trailer that said "60 feet ahead is our greatest asset." I immediately knew that the company meant that their driver was the most important thing but wondered how many people did not know what the quote was implying. Most trailers are around 53 feet long, and adding a few feet would land you on the driver's seat of the truck. See, I figured that there must have been some important cargo inside that trailer being towed by that very expensive rig, and without that driver safely operating the precious cargo, neither would make it to its destination.

The trucking company knew that it had to take care of and appreciate the employee held with the critical responsibility of transporting the load. They obviously wanted to make it known to the world that they appreciate their employees by writing it on the back of a trailer that travels across the country. The sentence on the trailer would also stay with that employee throughout her/his journey and serve as a reminder that their employer cared about them. I was pleased to have witnessed that meaningful mobile message.

The dictatorship times of leadership are a thing of the past and hold no weight anymore in any place of business. In a military or paramilitary organizations, such as a police department, orders are followed without questions by the troops. Fast-forwarding to current times, it is now important to include the troops in the mission of the organization and include them into why the orders are being given or changes are occurring. This is also true at home and in any place of business, not only paramilitary organizations.

When we were children and were told to do something by our parent, we asked "why," and the classic answer our parents gave us was, "Because I said so, that's why!" This practice nowadays will get you nowhere at work, and even if a change cannot occur for whatever given reason, it is important to let the employee know why it is not the right time for a change. If explained properly and closure is given to the employee on a change that cannot be implemented or if an unpopular change is put in place, then the employee will have no room for interpretation to gossip to coworkers on why it was or was not done.

Humans tend to get set in their ways, and employees may be weary of changes. Embracing and creating change will be discussed further in a later chapter. There is nothing wrong with having a professional conversation with an employee affected by an organizational change. I will later discuss further how adjusting your supervisory style to different generations is necessary and how the modern-day generation relish explanations.

I remember when I was in the running for a vacant sergeant's position and successfully scored highest on the promotional examination. The joy of the promotion after all the studying and preparation that was put in during the process was unexplainable. When preparing for a promotional exam, it is not only you that puts in the hard work. Your family must support the process, and undoubtedly, Lina picked up my slack around the house when I would lock myself up in a bedroom to study. As in everything else that I have ever done, she was supportive, and because of that, it was all worth it.

The morning after the test results were given, the former chief at the time called me into his office, and as I walked in, I could see a shiny gold badge sitting on the desk in front of him. He congratulated me, and after a short conversation, he slowly slid the badge in front of me and said, "Sarge, it's lonely at the top." I didn't really understand what he meant but did remember that he was not the type of leader that people flocked to, rather one that people avoided running into in the hallway. I knew that in my newly appointed supervisory position, I did not want employees to avoid me as this would continue to add to the cause of an undesirable workplace present.

Earlier in this book, I said that leaders are lifelong learners and you can learn from former bosses what to use and what to leave out of your supervisory style. In the case of my promotion encounter with the chief, I did not want it to be lonely for me at the top. I would later hear an instructor at a seminar that I attended say that he once came into a new company as a manager and that not one person had anything positive to say about the previous boss. The instructor said that he made it his mission to never be like the previous manager and to never make his employees feel unappreciated by a supervisor. My experience in receiving my shiny gold badge that my family and I worked so hard for was not what I expected but definitely a leadership learning experience.

The chief's office at the time was located on one end of the building along with the other command staff personnel. This also included a deputy chief, a captain, and a lieutenant's office. The sergeant's offices and police officer's roll call room was located on the far other end of the building. During the early days at the police department, whenever negative discussion of the command staff occurred, people used to point toward their wing of the building as if they were in another country. It almost represented division as in a "them versus us" setting. For the employees flying under the radar who didn't really want interaction with the bosses, this setting was ideal. I also discovered later that this was a bad layout for involving employees and interacting with them.

Years later, under the command of the new chief of police, I was promoted to operations lieutenant after working as a patrol sergeant as well as the detective bureau sergeant. I was excited and ready to take on a new journey in my new position. The position was different now, holding a new rank, but the mission remained the same. Much progress had already been made on our end of the building during my time as a sergeant, but we were still far from where we should have been.

I was now part of the command staff and was shown to my new office on the other end of the building by the chief. It was actually a very nice office, but something about it just didn't feel right. He asked me if I needed anything else, and I replied, "Yes, I need another office, please." He asked me if there was something wrong with this office, but I respectfully said that I would prefer to remain on the other side of the building. My request would not be the traditional placement layout for administrator's offices, but I was not asking for much. In actuality, the office that I was requesting was essentially smaller than the one that I was originally being offered. I was granted the office opposite of the command staff and closer to the troops, and it would later prove to be one of the most important first decisions that I made as a lieutenant.

During my days as a police officer, I remember one of the complaints from other officers and sergeants to be that they never saw administration personnel. That complaint ended when everyone had to walk by my open office when coming in and out of the building. This was a great time to quickly address issues as needed and interact with employees of every level. If there was nothing imperative to address, it was a good opportunity to have a humanistic conversation with employees.

If there was an issue of priority that needed to be addressed, I was fortunate to be located on the busy side of the building where most of our business was conducted. One of the biggest mistakes bosses make is to not quickly deal with issues pertaining to employees. Sometimes bosses will let some cool-off time go by before addressing an issue or, even worse, not deal with it at all. While some situations may merit a cool-off period, most need to be immediately addressed. This office was perfect. There were even times that employees would come to me with an issue without me even having to ask about it simply because I was there with them.

Looking back at my days working alongside my father at the telecommunications company, I remember him quickly addressing negative issues but not really always praising employees for good performance. I'm not bringing up my father because I believe he was doing it all wrong. I learned a lot from the old man, but just like all of us, there are things he could have done better. His lack of praising employees was probably just a sign of the generation where it was expected that you performed well and you only heard from the boss when something was wrong. That is no longer the case nowadays. The current generation wants to hear from their leaders and crave interaction, praise, and recognition from them.

Praise and recognition, though, is not simply saying "good job" at the end of the day, as I will discuss later. Some days, there is not a lot of contact with employees, and if you say good job to them, they may wonder what the heck you are "good jobbing" them for. Praise needs to be task specific, such as "good job on closing on that account today" or "thank you for being the top seller today." In police work, I was given a "good job" statement at the end of the day by supervisors that did not even see me during the entire shift.

Police canine dogs are a great example of how praise and reward assist in improving performance. If you only punish the canine and never reward them, they will not perform for you. Police dogs thrives on praise and need to be constantly rewarded for specific tasks performed, just as our employees do. Catherine Ponder says, "What you praise you increase." And I agree.

I remember one day during my early years as a lieutenant sitting in my office when a recently promoted sergeant walked by my office, and I called out his name as he whisked by. I invited him in for a chat about how things were going with him and his squad. He was so excited with his new position and expressed to me how challenging it was to work with a specific officer under his command. I let him vent as he explained some of the issues he was dealing with. I did my best to convey some positive feedback and suggestions regarding the employee. Most importantly, as he spoke of the inadequacies of the employee, what I was searching for was what the sergeant may or may not have been doing to stimulate the officer to modify his performance.

Without sounding obviously contrary to what the sergeant was saying, I articulated the fact that not everyone is good at everything and that we all have our own strengths and weaknesses, and I challenged him to search for the officer's strengths and attempt to amplify them. I used this meeting as an opportunity to praise the sergeant on how well a job he was doing and told him that he well-deserved the supervisor's position because of his work product as an officer. I added that not everyone possesses or even desires the traits and qualities of a supervisor. It was important that he immediately attempted to recognize the officer's qualities and venture toward learning what they are. Just as I had invited the sergeant in for a conversation to discuss the concerns in attempt to improve them, I suggested that he do the same with the officer.

I would later learn that as a result of a welcoming meeting between the two, the sergeant discovered that there were some functions performed within the organization that other officers had the opportunity to do that were never offered to him. The officer's pride would not allow him to speak up in the past, and he instead bottled it up, which supported his negative morale. Far too many times supervisors only address disciplinary matters with employees and fail to meet with them on good terms to simply commend employees and determine if there are issues consuming them. A supervisor must dig for what can be adjusted to improve an employee's performance and morale.

The undeniable fact is that a great leader must create a high performance culture and use every tool possible to improve morale within an organization. We need our employees to feel good at work, and if that outcome can be successfully achieved, then you will have already achieved your most important job as a leader. In corporate America, it is common when the restructuring of an underperforming company takes place to see upper level members lose their jobs first. The conception is that if the organization is not performing to standards and expectations, the leaders are ultimately held accountable.

We are put in leadership positions usually because of the preparations we make in our lives to be put in these positions and held responsible for keeping the position because of what we do while in them. If we fail to discover what employees desire in order to give high performance, then we will fail in our responsibilities as leaders. Becoming a leader and all the preparations it took to get there is about one's self. Being a true leader is no longer about you. It now becomes about everyone else in the organization that holds an oar in their hand and how much we can make each member row to propel the organization to greatness.

I once took a business trip to Tallahassee, Florida, with the chief of police, Luis Diaz, and our city's mayor, Yoiset De La Cruz. We brought along several employees to represent us at an annual cook-off event that occurs on one of the days of the week-long event. There were also several other cities represented at the event, and it was truly a great time to network and interact with other organizations similar to ours. I could see a couple of guys that were employed by a neighboring agency focusing on the way we interacted with our employees which made me curious as to what they were so intrigued with.

Sometime during the event, and at an appropriate time, I asked one of them if they were enjoying the event, and he responded cheerfully that he was. He then said something that was very important to me. With a smile of surprise yet confusion on his face, he said, "You guys are awesome! I can't believe how happy your employees seem and how great you guys get along with your chief and mayor!" He continued the conversation about how he had been observing our comradery and how you would never see that in his organization.

Unfortunately, the agency that he worked for, as he described, had "toxic" leadership in place, and sadly, he felt like he was not appreciated for the work he did. He further explained that the employees at his agency performed their duties in fear and that when they were around the leaders of the organization, they could not really be themselves. He told me that we were very lucky to have our leaders and wished that his were the same. I explained to him that in our agency, one hand washes the other and both hands wash the face. In other words, our leaders take care of and appreciate our employees, and in return, we take care of our leaders. Together, we take care of our organization and the people we serve.

This gentleman was obviously not satisfied with the leadership in place at his organization and was making a comparison between us and the way things were for him. You may be a leader that comes into an organization of this type or be a lower-level employee that works your way up the ladder to be in a leadership position that everyone will be watching to make the necessary changes. Although many advancements will not happen overnight, making the employees feel awesome is a simple task that can start on day one and will make a world of a difference in production and morale.

Ultimately, employees need to feel appreciated for what they do. Dutch author and inspirational speaker Alexander den Heijer quoted it best when he said, "When I talk to managers, I get the feeling that they are important. When I talk to leaders, I get the feeling that I am important." Employees are more than important, they are awesome. Show it by genuinely connecting with them.

Of course, there are leaders of very large organizations that cannot connect with each and every employee at all times. Some will make every effort to do what they can, considering the size of their organization. Even a small jester will be appreciated by employees. I once heard of a leader of an organization of around two thousand employees that would send a personalized e-mail greeting to three or four employees daily that they uncontrollably had little daily contact with. Throughout the year, every employee got to hear, in writing, how much they were appreciated by the big boss himself.

I also saw a video streaming through the Internet of Jeff Bezos, CEO of Amazon and Whole Foods, visiting fulfillment centers at both establishments during the COVID-19 pandemic. In the video, Bezos is seen wearing a protective mask while walking through the establishments thanking employees for their hard work. Because of the situation, he was not shaking hands and keeping a safe distance, but nevertheless, he was there on the grounds with them to show support rather than remaining distant and not physically showing encouragement during the trying time.

Employees need this type of support from their leaders. Employee engagement is very important and not to be confused with employee satisfaction. Employee/leadership engagement has been proven to reduce turnover. Most importantly, making employees feel appreciated makes them happy, which will have a trickling effect on other aspects of the organization. A manager that remains out of touch with their employees is unable to manage them properly.

While you need to keep a professional distance, maintaining a meaningful work relationship with employees will help you understand what motivates them. When employees feel in tune with their supervisor, they tend to be more invested in the work they are doing. This trait may not always come natural to a leader but can be developed with desire. Your team and your organization need you. Make employees feel awesome, and your organization will reap the benefits.

Chapter Three

Sometimes Your Coffee Has to Get Cold

If you hang around a crowded area and sit for a while listening to various conversations, you will hear the word "I" said more than any other word. If you sit and people watch in a busy foot traffic area, most people are mostly thinking about where they are going, what they need to do, and other things related to them. Truth is that we talk and think about ourselves and our priorities more than any other thing. Keeping that in mind in the workplace and knowing how interested we are in ourselves will assist the leader in effectively communicating with employees and making them feel important. Many organizations lack important interaction between its leaders and employees. Unfortunately, it is way too common for us as supervisors to get caught up in our own duties and fail to properly communicate with others.

In my organization, I practice a morning routine that has proven to be very valuable which I call "checking the pulse." Upon arriving to work, I first make my way to the coffee machine in the break room and pour my morning cup of Joe. Then, I begin making my rounds throughout all the departments and check pulses. What I mean by that is that I actually make contact with as many employees as possible and have a conversation preferably not work related. I begin with saying good morning, of course, then jump right in with a question or inquiry about the employee's personal life. If I know that someone's child was sick, I first ask how the child was doing and ask the question using the child's name if I know it.

The key to checking the pulse is to strike a conversation that would get the employee talking about themselves and their matters. If the conversation becomes work related, the contact is a win-win. The initiation of the conversation should focus on something other than work though. You should try to stay away from questions where you may get a one-word answer. If you ask, "How was your weekend?" you are sure to get an answer of "Good." It is better to ask a question that will get the employee talking, such as "So, what did you do on your time off" or "Tell me how it went on your trip."

The key to these interactions is to become genuinely interested in what is going on in the employee's world. If there was any advice I could give to assist the employee, I would use this opportunity to give it, and if there was not, at least they have this encounter to speak to me and bring up any issues that they wish to discuss including work-related issues that may need addressing. If you work for a rather large organization and cannot free up enough morning time, it's okay. Breaking up the staff into different days or even different times throughout the day will work just as well. The checking of the pulse routine has proven to make employees feel appreciated by their supervisors and should always be incorporated into a leader's duties.

Everyone possesses a need to feel appreciated, and when communicating with employees, we must listen attentively, paying attention to detail. Lou Holtz said, "In the successful organization, no detail is too small to escape close attention." In some conversations with employees, the devil is in the details. Pay attention to all that is said. There may be something not said that wants to get out, and if we do not listen attentively, we may miss it. Stephen Covey said it well. He said, "The single biggest problem in communication is we do not listen to understand. We listen to reply."

Encounters with employees can be viewed as your positive deposit into a bank account. You want to make sure your account is always fed, and you never want your balance to get too low. If some time has passed without making a deposit, then you run the risk of your account getting too low or, even worse, becoming negative. If this occurs, make sure to increase your balance in that employee by redepositing positive information into them. Because of other supervisory responsibilities, it is not hard to unknowingly neglect employees. When you have realized that this may have occurred, bounce back and catch up.

There should be some caution when communicating with employees. Humans have a tendency to create quarrels among each other when we are together for long periods of time. Knowing this, we must always be mindful as leaders to divert negative conversations about other coworkers, and we should never add to negative talk about another employee. I have heard supervisors too many times supplement negative comments during a conversation by saying things, such as "Yea, she or he is crazy" or "Yea, that's just the way she or he is." This is a leadership mistake and should never be done by a supervisor.

If an employee begins to speak ill of another employee, it is imperative that we tactfully make some sort of compliment about the other employee's strengths and remind them that everyone is different and we all possess strengths and weaknesses. The key is to never let any employee hear you speak negatively about anyone in the organization and let them know that everyone is an important piece to the organization's puzzle. Benjamin Franklin said it best when he said, "I will speak ill of no man and speak all the good I know of everybody." You will be amazed at how the conversation will transform form negative to positive, and the employee will soon know that there is no place in the organization for scolding and negative talk. With that, there is a saying in police work that says, "There are no secrets in a police department," and I know it goes the same for any other place of business. If there is negative talk about someone, chances are that it will get back to them.

The morning interactions were sometimes time-consuming but a good time to enjoy my morning coffee while feeling out employees and trying to assist in a good start to their day. More interactions would occur for me on a daily basis, especially now that my office was located where most of the employee traffic was. My office was cozy and inviting, and the door was always open. I made it a point when someone walked in to stand up and shake the person's hand and invite them to sit. I made it a point to never shake a hand while I was sitting down and would jokingly say to myself not to feel bad about skipping leg day at the gym because of this.

Greeting an employee should be performed the same way that you would greet a CEO, a potential client, or a person that you are meeting for the first time and are trying to make a good first impression. Giving a nice firm handshake, making eye contact, and saying the person's name when you greet them will show that you care and are welcoming of their presence. The key is to give every employee that you encounter from the CEO to the cleaning staff a star-quality greeting.

Sometimes when one holds a management position, they tend to only tell employees what to do and talk mostly about job functions with them. While there is a time and place for that, we, as leaders, must remember to always attentively listen. There's a saying that God gave us two ears and one mouth; therefore, we need to listen twice as much as we speak. Larry King said, "I remind myself every morning, nothing I say this day will teach me anything. So if I'm going to learn, I must do it by listening."

While I now had greater responsibilities holding a higher rank, I made it a point to always stop what I was doing and make eye contact with the visitor. All too many times bosses remain consumed in their work while communicating with an employee, and in this digitally electronic age that we are living in, it is becoming more common to type on a phone or computer keyboard as someone is speaking to you. I don't believe anyone can feel appreciated when they are talking to you and you are looking back and forth from a computer to them or texting while they talk. Full attention to the conversation must be given regardless of what it is about, and feedback must be given in order for the employee to know that you care and you are interested in what they are saying. If you pay attention at work or in your personal life, you will notice that this action unfortunately constantly occurs. When you find yourself in this situation, quickly correct it by turning away from your computers and laying your cellular phone face down on your desk. The results will be wondrous.

I remember one morning as I began my rounds of checking pulses just after pouring my cup of coffee. As I entered the communications center and began greeting the employees, one of them told me that there was a lady in the lobby that was upset because no one has been able to help her. After obtaining some information regarding her concerns, I sat my coffee cup down and proceeded to the lobby to attempt to assist her. I properly introduced myself, and she immediately began to complain about another police department who gave her information that she was not happy with. She said that they were short with her and quickly sent her on her way.

I listened to her concerns and quite frankly, the information that she was given by the other police agency was correct. I let her speak her mind for as long as she needed as I listened attentively until eventually she began to repeat the same information that she had already given me. She was all out of things to say but appeared content that I was showing concern. At an appropriate time during the conversation, I explained it to her in a different way and gave her valuably suggestions on what else she can do. She was now visibly more at ease than she was when I approached her. She thanked me for the information that I provided and went on her way.

As I returned to the communications center to continue my morning meets with the employees, one of them said, "Now your coffee is cold." I had been in the lobby for quite some time attempting to put the poor lady at ease, so now I was left with a cold cup of coffee but also a satisfied person that I was able to assist. The communications officer asked me if the lady was crazy, but I politely replied that she just wanted to express a concern and needed some information that fortunately I was able to give her. She again said, "Well, now your coffee is cold." I replied, "Sometimes your coffee has to get cold."

I took this opportunity to coach the communications officer and explain to her that people want to be heard and that sometimes we need to put stuff aside and tend to our customers. Everyone's issues are important to them, and if we can assist them at the cost of a coffee getting cold, then we have succeeded. We must train our employees and continue to train them at every encounter that merits training. Informal training and coaching should always be performed in situations such as this one, and we should never wait for an official training event to mentor them. The actions of a leader can be contagious and will be repeated by employees. We must make sure our actions are positive and benefit the organization, making a good impression on those that are watching.

Your coffee may also have to get cold when interacting with employees. While taking a sip of your coffee when someone is speaking to you may constitute as rudeness to some people, other tasks that you are physically working on may as well. As previously stated, rather than facing our computer or constantly looking at our phones during a conversation, sometimes tasks need to be put on ice for a few minutes while genuine attention is given to the person in front of you. Whether it results in your coffee getting cold or an assignment getting put off for a few minutes, your attention needs to be fully on the conversation. If you can successfully perform the simple task of giving full attention, then you will become a go-to person that employees will approach and want to speak to.

You want to be approachable as a leader and not one that employees avoid. Throughout all my experiences as a supervisor, for some reason, when employees call me on the phone, they start the conversation by saying "Sorry to bother you" then proceed with the reason for their call. This opening line should be immediately addressed by the supervisor by advising the employee that they are never a bother and should not start a conversation to you by implying that it is. Some employees feel like they are bugging a supervisor when contacting them. It needs to be made clear that they are never a bother and that you are there for them when they need you.

Sometimes You Have to Pour a Fresh Cup of Coffee

There will be times that you may need to pour a fresh cup of coffee and gather yourself before interacting with an employee. I was once given a task to complete by my captain and shortly after another given to me by the police chief. I was close to being overwhelmed because of the fact that I wanted to produce a result quickly for the both of them. Just at the moment of intensely focused production on the task, an employee entered my office and began to run something by me. I was almost rude when responding but remembered that I lived by an open-door policy. Instead, I politely asked that I get back to her because I was working on a time-sensitive project.

Once I was done with my task, I cleared my head for room for her affairs and made my way over to her office. On the way to her office, I made a stop at the coffee machine and poured two cups of coffee. Upon arriving to her office, I apologized for not addressing her affair more swiftly and gave her one of the cups of coffee. I added that I wanted to give her my undivided attention and that now we can discuss it over a cup of coffee. If for any reason she was not pleased in me for not previously tending to her issue, it was sure water under the bridge now.

Chapter Four

Embrace Change

Sometime in the early '90s, while sitting at my desk at KM Contacting, I can remember the vice president of the company, Ed Rose, wheeling in a big box that appeared to be a computer. He approached my desk and told me that the computer was for me and that we would now be transitioning to electronic forms and communicating more through e-mail. Given the times, I was so terrorized by the thought of learning how to operate this PC that my kids would laugh at me today if they saw me. What was I to do, say "No, Ed, I'm good, keep your stupid computer"? It definitely crossed my mind, but instead, I sucked it up, and after a brief tutorial, I began to master index finger only typing.

The desktop computer soon became one of my most important tools, and I actually began to incorporate some extra fingers into the typing. This outlandish device would later prove to be a very valuable tool as I will indicate later in this book. My computer story is sure proof that changes are inevitable whether it is technology, policies and procedures, and even changes in generations newly entering the workforce.

Knowing and expecting that changes will always come, I made sure that interpreting the changes that came from above was always done as positively as possible. Looking back on my days as an officer listening to the sergeant at briefing time, I can remember how terribly the sometimes inevitable changes were communicated. A supervisor rolling their eyes and talking about how horrible the new change was set the tone early for resistance to the change by the subordinates. I couldn't help but think back on the day that Ed brought in that weird machine and said, "Here's your computer!" I also thought about how he sold me on the idea that I was going to love having it and how much easier our job was going to be now. Ed's positive delivery motivated me to want to learn how to use it, but my reaction would have been totally different had he expressed himself negatively on the new device.

We need to learn to accept that change within an organization is usually good, and our delivery when presenting it must be done positively. Changes are constant in our personal lives, and that is why we continuously see it going on around us, such as changes in fashions and hairstyles. Most of us avoid stagnation in our personal lives but freak out when changes are implemented at work. Adaptation to change will be sure to come, and we have to explain that to employees affected by the change. It's sort of like moving from one home to another. At first, the new home is out of order, but before you know it, everything falls back into place.

As leaders, we need to be bold enough to foster change and encourage positive buy-in from the employees affected by the changes. In some cases, the change will actually be correcting a function that has previously been performed improperly. I remember when I was newly promoted to sergeant and would attempt to correct something that was being performed incorrectly, countless times employees would say one of my least favorite comment, "That's the way we've always done it." Well, just because a task has been performed a certain way does not always mean that it has been performed correctly. A true leader must be bold enough to get people out of their comfort zone and out of a habit of incorrect performances.

By politely asking the employee to try to perform a task a different way, you will get a better response. Make it clear that you are not a new person coming into power that wants to shake things up. If you barge into a new position like an old Western movie ranting "There is new sheriff in town," you will sure be met with resistance. The desired result will more than likely be received based on your delivery.

Making changes within an organization can be especially difficult for newly promoted employees and may at times be met with resistance. It must be made clear when implementing change that the changes are for the betterment of the organization. Employees need guidance and support and need to be advised why the change is important and must feel confident that supervisors are there for them during and after the changes are implemented. The positive delivery of change and feeling of support by supervisors will have an immense impact on the organization's employees.

One of the most difficult changes to address is that of a toxic employee. We all know them, and most of us have them in our organizations. As leaders, we must make sure to quickly address toxicity which, as we all know, can spread like a wildfire. I have always made it a point to not fuel negative conversations by adding to the negativity. Look at a conversation as nourishment for your mind and avoid taking in harmful toxins from coworker's words. Divert the conversation to something positive whenever possible after letting the employee know that toxic behavior is not accepted.

I see it all the time as a customer in stores when employees that represent the store are serving me and at the same time speaking negatively about the store. I remember one case in particular when I was at a checkout lane at a grocery store, and I asked the cashier how she was doing. She rolled her eyes as she began to tell me how bad things were there and that it seemed to be getting worse every day. She continued on and on about how terrible the manager was and how awful the work conditions have become. Quite honestly, I was not impressed.

While listening to her complain, it was obvious that she was dissatisfied with her place of employment and that there was a big possibility that inadequate leadership may have been in place. I simply said to her that we are very lucky to have jobs and reminded her how difficult job hunting is when we are out of work. I made only another few more positive comments before our conversation took a different path. Hopefully, the next customer in line was met with a different attitude as a result of our conversation transition.

In another similar situation shortly after being seated at a busy restaurant, a young waiter approached our table and initiated the conversation by apologizing in advance if his service is not up to par but that he was handling several tables at once. I replied by asking him if they were short-staffed as a result of someone calling out sick. He answered that no one had called out and that it is not uncommon for him to handle several tables at once because as he stated, "That is just how it is here." He added that the manager expects them to wait on several tables and must think that "We are robots." I gave him a friendly smile and used the same tactic that I gave the cashier in the previous incident. I started by giving him positive reinforcement that I was sure he would do a great job and added that he was fortunate to have all the tables to receive the gratuities for himself.

As the waiter took my drink order, I continued our conversation by telling him that he was making it all look so easy and that he appeared confident in his job. I continued throughout our encounter with some positive words coupled with praise for his great service. By the time the bill came, our conversation had turned positive and not one more time did he mention a negative comment about his work environment. The key point is that I, only as a customer, made a positive impact on the conversations during the short encounters with the two employees. An immediate supervisor that spends more long periods of time with employees should be able to modify mentality so that customers do not experience what I did on the two encounters.

As supervisors, if we address change and negative behavior properly and foster a positive work environment, it will become second nature to the employee and be demonstrated to customers through them. The last thing that any organization needs is for their frontline women and men to bad-mouth the very place that they work for and relay negative thoughts about the organization to the customers. You can very easily get around negative feelings by your delivery during a change or your reaction to negative comments. Master it, and it will, too, become second nature.

Many leaders do not realize that they may be the cause of negative employee output. Leaders must properly train and prepare employees and not set them up for failure at the front line. I'll give you a perfect example. When I was registering for my PhD and going through all the entry requirement, I naturally had some questions for the institution and called them several times throughout the process. Every time I called, I spoke to a different representative, and each and every one of them were just as pleasant to speak to and properly addressed my issues. It was obvious that they received some pretty great training by the way they treated me.

I noticed after speaking to multiple representatives on various different calls that they all had a similar format to addressing my questions and concerns. One method that stood out, and was very impressive, was when they needed to put me on hold for any reason, they always asked me if I could hold for a specific number of minutes. If they asked me if I could hold for three minutes, they always came back on the line to check on me in exactly three minutes. If they asked me if I could hold for four minutes, they always came back on the line in exactly four minutes. It is as if they had a timer that prompted them at the time they said they would get back to me. Even if they had not yet had the answer for me, they would come back and advise me of such then ask if I could be placed on hold again for another specific number of minutes.

While it seemed like a simple thing to do, it kept me constantly informed of what was going on and made me feel valued. I was never put on hold for long periods of time listening to "hold music" or an audio recording of someone talking about how important my call was to them. The management of this particular institution realized that people in general do not like waiting, so they came up with this procedure to put callers at ease. A result was a happy and informed caller that did not take his holding frustrations out on the frontline employee.

Be a Change Agent

Lack of progress as a result of stagnation is the slow death of any organization, but many organizational members are usually resistant to change, which can make being a change agent that much more challenging for a leader. As a change agent, you will need to alter the organizational norms in order for the organization to advance. Change efforts should always be aligned with the organization's mission and strategic plan but never should a leader become motionless themselves when it comes to implementing change.

When I started at my police agency, I was issued a three-inch three-ring binder containing the general orders, policies, and rules of the police department. To my surprise, they were dated approximately twenty years before the current date and had a former police chief's name all over them. While some things probably hadn't changed, I know that some of the stuff contained in there must have been outdated. Several years later when the agency was seeking accreditation status, the outdated policies obviously had to be updated.

Had the agency not pursued accreditation status, Lord knows how long we would have been operating under antique policies. It is a leader's responsibility to identify flaws in the policies, procedures, and operational functions of an organization and attempt to make changes as needed. Steve Jobs is a perfect example of a change agent with an incredible vision for Apple. He constantly challenged his employees and made it clear in what direction he wanted to move the company. He changed the way the company did business and propelled the organization to amazing success.

If you are anything like me, you have to write things down or you will forget them. As a dedicated leader, ideas to better the organization would come to mind when I was not at work, and I would quickly make a note of it for future implementation. Fortunately, I discovered the "notes" application in my smartphone and filled it up with ideas. If you are a motivated first-in-last-out leader, ideas will just come to you whatever method you use, whether it is writing it down or recording a voice memo on your smartphone, document it, and begin to come up with an implementation strategy.

Ultimately, making cultural changes in an organization is a long and arduous process, but acting on needed changes may save the company from indolent demise. Included in implementing change, a change agent must include appropriate interpretation of changes to employees, properly convincing them that the change is needed and being done for the betterment of the organization and its members. Again, resistance will be present in some. Deal with it properly and continue on with the goal.

Inevitable Change

As earlier discussed, change is inevitable. I have supervised the operations of a telecommunications company that serviced utilities and also the operations of a police department. Both organizations were located in South Florida where hurricanes seemed to almost be a normal thing. You can imagine how normal operations will be turned upside down when a hurricane hits. Employees responsible for servicing utility lines after a hurricane as well as police officers held with the tasks that come with a disastrous storm will both be faced with a change in normal duties as well as an exhausting recovery effort. The changes in duties and time away from families can be stressful and must be recognized by a leader.

As it will be discussed later in this book, employees need to feel the support from the top during crisis and inevitable changes and must be recognized for their work. The changes, which may not always be welcomed by everyone, need to be presented as a goal to be accomplished and that the goal cannot be accomplished without them. Employees must be told that they are an important part of the organizational puzzle during the change in assignments and tasks, and a leader must deliver this message so that the employees embrace the change that is presented.

Change was evidently shocking during the COVID-19 pandemic, and people were required to do something that they would not normally do. It seemed very strange at first to see people out and about with surgical masks until eventually it did not seem so outrageous. Now, this is definitely seen as an extreme change, but people adapted because they were explained the reason for protecting themselves and complied. When your team is faced with changes, they, too, will go through phases, and it is no one else's responsibility but the leader's to guide them through the inevitable changes.

Chapter Five

Foster Leadership

While it was said in the introduction, and will be discussed again later, that leaders are made, not born, everyone is born with leadership qualities that can be developed through life experiences and motivators that will bring out the qualities within. One of the biggest mistakes leaders make is to hold on to too much responsibilities and not build employees by empowering them to do a variety of duties performed in an organization. Former CEO of General Electric, Jack Welch, said, "Before you are a leader, success is all about growing yourself. When you become a leader, success is all about growing others." That means that leadership is in part an act of persuading others to be leaders.

Several years ago, I attended an accreditations assessor's course in Punta Gorda, Florida, and remember the chief of police at the time, Albert (Butch) Arnel, starting the class with some opening statements. He wasn't teaching the class, rather welcoming us to his agency and thanking us for attending. Butch, as he requested to be called, said something that stuck in my head that was very inspiring. He introduced the two instructors, a lieutenant and a captain, and said that he was heading out of town for a business meeting but that we were in good hands. He added that if the lieutenant and captain professors needed anything, they knew they could call him, but he was pretty sure that they were not going to. He continued on saying that the two were able to totally run the agency without him because that's what he had prepared them to do in his absence.

Butch added that he is never impressed at meetings when he sees other police chiefs constantly walking outside to use their phones to conduct business that could probably not be done without them. The leaders that Chief Arnel had in place were prepared by him to perform all the duties of the agency in his absence. This was as a result of his doing, and I'm pretty sure it did not happen overnight. Chief Arnel would later continue his career as again an influential chief at a different police department.

Training future leaders should not be thought of as something that occurs in a classroom. Informal training sessions should be part of a leader's everyday life. We should always make the time to develop people by helping them learn and improve. Many managers unfortunately fail to do this. Some employees receive very little training after employed, and as stated earlier, leaders are lifelong learners; therefore time must be put into the development of our future leaders.

Unfortunately, many executives see training and development as an added expense for the organization. The mentality of not training employees because of costs can be more costly in the long run. When you invest money and time into your people, they are likely to feel of value to the organization and stay. When they don't feel valued, they are more likely to leave to a company that values and invests in them. Regardless, failure to train will result in mediocre performance which can be more costly in the long run. Henry Ford said it best when he said, "The only thing worse than training your employees and having them leave is not training them and having them stay."

Sadly, I have known supervisors that have harbored knowledge of certain functional tasks within an organization almost as to illustrate that without them, the show will not go on and the ship will sink. This is a major supervisory error and perhaps a way to try to secure a position. This sort of task knowledge harboring is not needed if one is performing their responsibilities satisfactorily. Rather than having full control and knowledge of certain duties, a true leader will prepare a subordinate to move into their position and work toward advancing themselves to the next level.

For many of my years as a supervisor and even as a parent, I possessed the flaw of measuring other people's motivation and performance to the same caliber as mine. I automatically assumed that everyone, even my kids, knew everything that I knew and should be seeing things the way that I did. Preparing employees to move into your position when you move up within the organization takes time and work just as it does to raise children and teach them what they need to know throughout the years. Randy Pausch, the author of *The Last Lecture*, wrote the book and gave his famous lecture at Carnegie Mellon University to teach his children the lessons that he learned during his life. Unfortunately, Randy wrote the book after being diagnosed with pancreatic cancer, knowing that he may not be around to teach his kids these valuable lessons.

There are supervisors that move up in an organization and hold on to tasks pertaining to their prior roll. They fail to pass on the responsibilities to the employee occupying their position. They either have a feeling of ownership in the task or feel that it will get accomplished better if they do it. Either way, it is a supervisory mistake and a failure to foster leadership. While it may be hard to let go of a task, a leader needs to guide and mentor future leaders and create some space between them and their prior duties, allowing others to perform them.

While you can and should learn from others' mistakes, the best lessons are learned by that of experiences and failures. I know good and well that I have made mistakes, but mistakes have made me. As much as I want to guide my children and hold their hand through life, I know that without experiencing issues on their own, they will not truly learn lessons. With employees, I make it certain to give them the tools needed, a little care and motivation, and send them on their way to conduct functions on their own regardless of the outcome. The outcomes can later be learned from and looked at for future improvements.

Mistakes are made to be learned from, and if you spend most of your time as a manager micro-managing every little task, then building your employee's leadership skills will be surely delayed. As I have explained to my children that they will best learn from their mistakes, I have also let them know that they must self-reflect on ways to improve at every encounter they face. Gibbs' Reflective Cycle will be discussed later which outlines learning by doing which is the best concept for reflecting on experiences one has had and learning from them.

To be in a position to be able to help people grow and explore their potential is a privilege. Fostering leaders should be seen as nourishing to the mind of a potential future leader and help bring out leadership qualities that are unbeknownst to them hidden inside of them. We become the energy that influences drive and motivation in others. It will be easier for some than others as some have already developed some leadership qualities on their own and are naturally more motivated than others to improve themselves.

Through my supervisory experiences, I quickly discovered that not everyone had the desire and motivation to perform at the ultimate level. For this reason, I created the stairway of motivation theory.

At work, I imagine a large staircase that leads up to the top step which symbolizes ultimate drive and motivation. I grade each employee by how high on the staircase of motivation they are on and began to work on getting them to the next step. It would be a great mistake to expect that all employees will climb the stairs at the same speed. Some even come into the organization on a higher stair than others already employed there, and that's okay.

When I moved into a lieutenant's position, I did realize though that I began to lose touch with the officers on the field as I now had new duties that excessively preoccupied my time. But that never stopped me from making time to visit each of them and check their pulse to get a feel for any issues that needed addressing. It eventually dawned on me that the sergeants that immediately supervised them held one of the most important positions in the entire organization. The sergeants were the ones working alongside of them, boots on the ground, day in and day out, and had the most influence on them. My focus soon became to develop the sergeants and make sure that they had a positive impact on their teams. I now had to make sure that the personnel with the closest interaction with those that served the public (our customers) were properly motivated, trained, and taken care of.

In business, CEOs and upper management personnel are very influential but eventually have limited influence on the ground troops. It is important for upper management to focus largely on their organizations' supervisors to make sure that they are properly supervising the personnel that are performing the duties of the company. Rising through the ranks within an organization can be difficult when one's influence becomes limited to the ground troops and the baton is being passed down to someone else that will hold most of the stock in the impact that is being made in the employees.

When holding a higher position in an organization, many actions, be they positive or negative, can affect employees. One day, as a sergeant, at the end of a shift, I was entering the police station, and a new lieutenant sparked a conversation while walking into the building with me. It was well-known by all that at the end of a shift, the sergeants sit at a certain desk in the police station designated for sergeants to review electronic reports written by officers throughout a shift. The lieutenant, during midsentence, quickly sat at the desk, clearly hindering my duties. I shuffled some paperwork near the desk and stood aside him, hoping that he would realize that I needed to sit there. I eventually was politely blunt and asked him if I could have a seat to check some time-sensitive reports.

The lieutenant's reply shocked me. In a cocky way, he said, "Sarge, I just sat down. You're going to have to wait."

His actions and demeanor reflected that of a tyrant clearly dictating that he outranks me and that I would have to wait until he is good and ready to get up and that there was nothing I could do or say about it. It was saddening that he would delay my duties for a proving of power. It actually did the opposite. I would love to tell you that I lost respect for him, but quite honestly, until this point, he had not really yet earned the respect of anyone in the organization.

Fast-forward a few weeks later and at the beginning of a shift, as I enter the police station, I see the police chief sitting at the same desk (used by sergeants only) speaking to a couple of the early-arriving officers. As soon as the chief saw me walking down the hall, he quickly sprung up out of the chair and said, "What am I doing, this is where the sergeants sit?" In actuality, this particular desk was used by sergeants during the later hours to check reports and not usually used at the beginning of a shift. That didn't stop the chief from quickly getting up upon seeing me approaching. The chief did this not only in my presence but in the presence of patrol officers that were sitting around waiting for me to conduct my morning briefing.

Two different people in two different leadership positions and two very different actions. My immediate supervisor decided to take a seat and not get up even when kindly asked to do so in order for an organizational duty to be performed. On the contrast, the CEO and highest-ranking person in the agency practically jumped out of a seat and showed respect for the individual that it was created for without even being asked to. This small action had a huge impact on my views of two very different types of leaders. The simple action the chief showed that day by getting up gained him more respect by me and the troops, and the lieutenant's respect level remained nonexistent.

There are several ways to foster leadership by our actions alone. The actions witnessed by employees will be influential and repeated by them, causing a better work environment. Simply standing up to shake someone's hand or introducing a visitor to the cleaning lady will show respect and further build respect within the organization. A person's actions will tell you everything you need to know. As said by John Maxwell, "Actions are remembered long after words are forgotten."

As leaders, when creating other leaders, it is important to guide them in the right direction and teach them to be a people-person type leader. At our police agency, there were times where we would attend multiagency events where command staff personnel were present from other agencies. There was a police major from another agency at several events that always seemed to let the rank get to his head. He would greet me but never really interact much and sort of appeared to seem as if he was better than everyone else. Having met this sort of supervisor before, I really played it no mind.

That police major would eventually get into some trouble at his agency and be asked to resign. Having exchanged phone numbers with him in the past, to my surprise, I received an out-of-the-blue text message from him stating that he hopes all is well with me and my family and was just texting to say hi.

I also received a "Happy Easter" text on Easter day. This was out of the usual character for the major who will obviously remain nameless. I was later told by another command staff member at my agency that he, too, had received a similar text from the major.

Now, I'm no rocket scientist nor a betting man, but I figured that the major may have had some desire to get hired with us and had now become Major Friendly. That is exactly what happened. Some weeks later, I heard that he was inquiring about a possible opening with our organization. Unfortunately, there were no openings at the time.

A fine line is present, though, with employee engagement and close supervision. As leaders, we must trust our employees and allow them to perform on their own as much as possible. It is okay to take small breaks from meetings and e-mails to allow for employees to think for themselves. Setting too many deadlines and constantly asking for feedback can sometimes lead to the employees refraining from completing their own task to answer your e-mail or meet your deadline. An important method is to trust our employees to complete tasks and verify that they are being completed without constantly overwhelming them with additional tasks.

As leaders, we have to give employees the tools and ability to produce. Some supervisors will delegate their own duties to subordinates or tie them down to one particular assignment, and when things go bad in another area, they go up in arms, pestering the employees and questioning why productivity is dropping in the other area. If you encounter an employee that has a deficiency in one area of her or his assigned duties, prior to inquiring about it, conduct a quick self-evaluation to determine if maybe you are the cause of inadequacy. If you are in fact the cause, then regroup, restructure your delegating, and reevaluate the way you distribute assignments.

Now, delegation is okay when it is properly administered. Delegation should focus on empowerment. Empowering employees and being available to them for guidance without micromanaging is difficult for many supervisors. An empowerment failure can be either because too much responsibility is put on an employee with no guidance or feedback given or because of the unwillingness of a leader to give up responsibilities. The main result of empowering should be to create mutual trust. When there is trust up and down the chain of command of an organization, it makes it that much stronger.

If you ask any leader where they picked up their leadership qualities, they will more than likely tell you that they learned them through work experiences and from previous bosses. Whether positive or negative actions witnessed, they picked up the positives and left out the negatives. Very rarely will a leader say that they learned leadership through schooling or formal training. For that reason, if you are leading a team, you have a moral leadership obligation to develop more leaders. While formal training events do come in handy, the main source of leadership development will come from other leaders.

The next generation of leaders must be identified and developed. Since I repeatedly say that leaders are made, not born, we need to create the leaders that will catapult the organization to the next level and enhance the company's traditions to the modern-day ways. Many organizations hold on to an old vision and mission and fail to realize that the up-and-coming generation of leaders are the ones that will make positive and up-to-date changes that the new workforce coming in can relate to. However, new leaders and employees, while being allowed to be innovative, should still be in sync with vision and mission of the organization.

Chapter Six

Like a Marriage

Most people decorate their offices and work areas with pictures of their families and personalize the area with a little piece of themselves. The fact is that we spend much of our lives at work, and it somewhat becomes our second home. At our place of business, just as in our homes, we create relationships and quarrels with coworkers and realize what is required to get along with each other. Some will unify both homes through social gatherings, and nearly all of us involve our families in events that occur at work. My wife, Lina, always makes it a point to ask how work was and can always tell when I was dealing with an issue at work just by my demeanor when I walked in the door.

As a police officer, there are days that involve horrific events, and Lina could usually identify when a day like that occurred without me speaking a word of it. Not all professions see the worst things that occur in society as police officer do, but many occupations deal with a plethora of worrying issues that should be of concern to leaders of organizations. Leaders need to identify potential issues that can be addressed so that employees are not negatively impacted to the point that these issues are being brought home with them. The impact that work stressors can cause at home may mean big troubles for employees' drive and performance.

As leaders, we can eventually tell when employees are dealing with personal issues that may be affecting work product and morale, and it is important to create at work an open door to speak of issues as my wife has done at home. It dawned on me one day that my wife knew several employees' names that she had never met but would speak of them as if she has known them for years. Lina's involvement in my profession and the inevitable issues that occur when you are working with people was therapeutic in the sense that she was open to listen to my thoughts on specific issues and gave positive feedback without judging or blaming.

This natural trait possessed by my wife is a great tool that could be mirrored at work and was later used several times by me. When we pay attention to our employees and genuinely care for them, we will soon, too, be able to identify when there are issues of concern right when they walk in the door. I know that for me personally, having my wife identify when there was something going on out of the ordinary made me feel cared for. I am sure that employees will have the same feeling when you have identified it in them.

I remember an old friend talking to me about personal relationships and explaining that it is usually around the time when you have seen every item of clothing of a person that you are dating that the arguments and differences begin to occur. The fact remains that differences are inevitable with the people that we spend much of our time with. I remember my mother saying that my father gets along and treats everyone else differently than he did her. The reason for that was simply because of the amount of time that he spent with her and the changes that occur in personalities when we are around each other for an extended amount of time.

Marriages require discipline and commitment, and we must recognize this and expect that, regardless of what type of business our organization conducts, personality issues will arise. We must, just like at home, learn how to live and function with each other to create an environment where a healthy work relationship can foster and last.

In a marriage, loyalty, trust, and keeping your word is an essential recipe for a healthy and lasting relationship. In business, if you cook with the same recipe that makes a relationship last, you are likely to get the same in return from your employees. It will rub off on everyone around you and likely to be repeated by them. These traits are an absolute must, and your leadership success relies on your loyalty, trustworthiness, and your word.

I taught my kids about these important traits at a young age. I remember one day, right before one of my son Wesley's basketball games, I offered him an incentive. I wanted him to step up his rebounds, so I offered him twenty dollars for every rebound he got during the game. By his fourth rebound, I started to wonder if I should have offered him five bucks instead of twenty. He hustled his butt off like never before and ended the game with five rebounds, costing me one hundred dollars.

Shortly after we got home from the game, I walked into my son's room and handed him the hundred bucks. His humbleness didn't allow him to accept it, but I made him take it and told him that I was a man of my word. He said that he felt bad because he had, without me knowing, told a taller teammate that usually gets most of the rebounds to let him get some and that he would pay him twenty dollars once he was paid. I didn't really get mad at him for that and respected his hustle. The next day at practice, Wesley walked right up to his teammate accomplice and handed him his cut. I overheard him tell the boy, "Here you go because I'm a man of my word.". I couldn't have been prouder that he repeated my actions and kept his word.

As a leader, keeping your word will go a long way. That long way is what's necessary to prove your loyalty and trust. The key is contact. It is not uncommon for supervisors to get tied up with upper management duties and lose contact with employees. If you have ever been in a serious relationship, you know that a lot of interaction and communication is required. Actively listening to employees can tell you a lot about them and how they feel about a particular issue or job task. Mastering the function of listening can greatly help your professional relationship with employees.

As in the home, it is also important to quickly address issues at work. The old saying between husband and wife says never go to sleep in a fight. Issues need to be discussed and addressed in a timely manner and moved on from. At work, if an issue is not addressed quickly, it may have negative results. Nipping a problem in the bud can assist that it does not spread out of control like a wildfire within the organization. An open-minded discussion allowing for the employee to honestly speak their mind can become water under the bridge and moved on from toward a more productive action.

Michael Jordan said it best. He said, "The game is my wife. It demands loyalty and responsibility, and it gives me back fulfillment and peace." There were many reasons that Michael Jordan continued to play under Pat Riley for so many years. I'm sure one of the main reasons was because of Coach Riley's outstanding leadership but much had to do with Jordan's loyalty to his coach and team. A marriage should have a "we" mentality and should never be about yourself. The same can be thought of in the leadership of personnel within every organization.

I do have to admit though that I have led hundreds of employees throughout my two decades in management, and the most difficult place for me to perform at being a leader is at home. For some reason, dealing with subordinates at work and motivating them came easier to me than at home with my family. I have had to focus more on how to get a positive response from my home family as where with my work family it comes easier. If you are a leader that finds one easier than the other, work diligently on flourishing at the one you lack in.

Family should give you stability, and you are the one that makes the ultimate decision whether to stay and work things out when the going gets tough or run off and avoid the struggle. But if you are willing to stay and work at it, you will soon find that family is the compass that guides us. Molding a healthy work family will result in the cultivation of a unified workforce where employees feel like they are as safe as they are in their home. If you are willing to put in the work, the results will be gratifying.

Just as in all other aspects of a healthy family, honesty is a main key ingredient. Employees will eventually know when you are an honest leader or simply one that blows smoke up their ass. Sometimes, leaders will fill employees' heads up with information that sounds as if the issue will benefit them, when in actuality, it will benefit only the organization or the leader himself. But time will get that type of leader discovered. With time, all true intentions will be revealed, and you can only fool someone for so long.

One of my superstar employees approached me once with a heavy heart and look of sorrow in his eyes and requested to speak to me. He broke the news to me that sadly, he had decided to take a job offer with another organization. I had to admit, I was truly shocked and immediately wondered what the underlying issue was for his decision. His reason was, unfortunately, something beyond my control. He had reached a peak in pay with us and had some personal issues that required more money.

When he explained to me the job offer details and the compensation that he will receive, I could not give him anything other than encouragement. Quite honestly, it was a great offer and truly one that he would be a fool to pass up. I decided to take this opportunity to conduct an exit interview, something that I do with all employees parting ways with our organization. His only reason for the decision was the money, and there were no possible strings that I could pull to match the deal that he was given. I gave him my honest opinion and told him that it was a great deal and that if he was going to better himself by taking the offer, he would have my full support.

Unfortunately for him, something didn't pan out, and he didn't get the job. Fortunately, for my organization, we got to keep this superb employee. Another meeting was conducted regarding sticking around. At this meeting, I reassured him that we would never hold anything against him for deciding to leave us and that we were sad for him that he didn't get the job, but we were blessed to keep him. I made sure that he knew that he was like family and that I would always support him and give him my honest opinion. Even if it meant losing him.

Several months later, an issue occurred between him and a coworker that he asked my advice on. I gave him my honest opinion. Some of which he probably didn't expect to hear. Regardless, my opinion was honest and one that I believed would benefit him and not just the one that he wanted to hear. I reminded him about when he wanted to leave and how I supported him because I knew it would benefit him. I used this opportunity to let him know that it would have benefitted me and the organization if he didn't leave, though I still gave him my honest opinion. In this case, he may have not liked my opinion regarding the quarrel between him and his coworker. Nevertheless, he now knew that whatever input he asked me to give would always be my honest opinion.

Just as in a relationship, trust, loyalty, and honesty take time to prove. Encounters over a long period of time show true colors. One can only put up a facade for so long before relationship troubles begin. Just as with family, every situation has to appropriately be addressed with proper guidance given to employees. Once you are identified by employees as this type of leader, you will begin to truly be compensated with trust, loyalty, and honesty in return.

Chapter Seven

Motivation

One of the main goals of a leader must be to motivate employees so that they always give their very best. Motivation and praise are something that must never be forgotten and constantly administered. Zig Ziglar said, "People often say that motivation doesn't last. Well, neither does bathing. That's why we recommend it daily." That quote could not be truer. Motivation is a function that is never completely achieved, so leaders should make sure to always check the motivation climate in their organization and come up with various ideas to keep employees motivated.

Motivation just tends to fade. My younger sons, Wesley and Ryan, were jiujitsu practitioners at a very young age. They competed in several matches growing up, usually taking first place at every competition. All my friends, family, and coworkers knew about their jiujitsu achievements, more than likely because I never shut up about it. I was very proud of them and would constantly boast about it.

To my surprise, one day they just decided that they no longer wanted to train or compete in jiu-jitsu. Naturally, I was crushed. After so many years of training and competing, the drive just stopped. I couldn't understand it and dreaded someone asking me about how their jiujitsu was going. I tried everything I could to keep them involved and interested to no avail. It was something that I never thought would happen, but the reality was that they were done with the sport.

My coworker, Vinny, would always ask me about the boys' competitions, and I would in return ask him about his son, Vinny Jr.'s baseball career. Vinny Jr. was quite the baseball player in high school and was sure to get a college scholarship with the extraordinary skills he had on the diamond. Baseball was their family's life, but to Vinny's surprise, his son also lost the aspiration to go pro and eventually quit the sport. Vinny and I had a lot in common when it came to our kids. They were all-stars that sadly lost motivation for a sport.

You could only imagine that if a few all-star boys can lose motivation at a sport, then employees can easily lose theirs too. You can ask anyone, and they'll probably agree that a sport is more entertaining than a job. The neurotransmitter that release dopamine are surely more functional during a sport than while performing a job task. However, work motivations can be related to sports motivations in a way by celebrating goal accomplishments and small successes. There has to be a vision of successful accomplishments in sports and work alike and a reason to wake up in the morning and get going. This ultimately has to be created by the leader.

Mornings in my home were always adventurous. Getting our kids ready for school was always an interesting task for Lina and I. The boys were the most challenging being that it was always hard to wake them up for school. During my son Wesley's first year of high school, he found himself a lady friend that he was interested in, and things changed overnight. The morning mission to wake him up and perform morning routines such as having breakfast and brushing his teeth instantly changed. He now had a reason to wake up in the morning.

Wesley was now motivated and had a reason to quickly get ready in the morning. His girlfriend was usually dropped off at school early by her parents and sat all alone until Wesley arrived. Wanting to spend every possible minute with her, he asked me to start dropping him off earlier than usual so that he can spend more time with her. To my surprise, Wesley started waking up on his own, and by the time I woke up, he would be all ready to go, looking and smelling good, of course.

There was now a motivating factor that had him up and going bright and early. Unfortunately, motivations fade and just as Wesley eventually began to slowly revert back to his old ways of sleeping in, employees, too, will lose motivation, drive, and desires. Before that occurs, a leader must come up with new motivators to keep the upbeat drive in employees. It is our duty and responsibility to do so. Faded motivation is a natural effect in humans, and just like taking vitamins that our bodies lack, we must prescribe motivation to employees as needed.

We need to create a workforce of worker bees, not flies. If you want to gather bees (workers), feed them honey; otherwise, you may end up with flies, which are usually attracted to shit. A great leader is approachable and makes people around them feel good about themselves. In order to motivate, employees must desire to be around you and never avoid your presence.

Be the honey leader, not the one that attracts flies. Honey is sweet, and people like it. Improved performance will occur when employees are administered something that feels good. What can we nourish employees with so that they feel motivated? For starters, compliment and praise are a couple of effective and very important methods that go a very long way. We all like to look and feel good, and regardless of what some say, we all care about ourselves and thrive for compliments and praise. Want proof? Have you ever been part of a group photo? When you look at the photo, who is the first person you look for? Yourself, of course! We want to make sure we look good, then we glance at the others in the photo. We might even ask the photo taker to take another one if we didn't like how we looked, regardless of how everyone else looks.

As a police officer, friends and family have always been intrigued by my line of work. At family gatherings, there is no way around the question "How's work?" People want to hear crime-fighting stories, and quite honestly, most police officers would rather not talk about work. This is an easy fix. A short answer and then a couple of questions about them will get them going, and more than likely, they will not ask too much more about you. Returning the question and asking how their job is going or asking a more specific question may be the end of their interest in you.

Whether they admit it or not, your employees crave attention and recognition. It starts when we are very young and is part of our DNA. When my boys were very young and one would do something brave, I would tell them how brave they were. My daughter, Abigail, the youngest, would ask if she was brave too even though she didn't perform the act that deserved the recognition. She would hear me praising her brother and wanted reassurance that I thought she was brave too. Now this doesn't mean we have to compliment and praise employees for something they didn't do. It proves that we all have a desire to feel important and told that we are.

In most all organizations, there are many members that deserve the praise for the job they do and others that supervisors struggle to motivate. As leaders, we must accept the fact that not all personnel in your organization will be on board with the vision and mission. Through my experiences, around 25 percent of employees are committed and fully on board with the mission of the organization and another 25 percent are not. The other 50 percent can be swayed to either side. A true leader will work diligently to keep the 25 percent that are on board motivated and use every method possible to pull in the 50 percent that can easily be drawn to either side.

Motivation consists in part of building someone up so that they have a full desire to complete a task. It also includes making someone feel like the task can be successfully accomplished. I bought my son, Wesley, a basketball hoop to keep out on the driveway of our home, and occasionally, I would join him for a one-on-one. When he was out there at times just shooting some hoops on his own, he would ask me, "Dad, you think I could make it from here?" I would answer "yes." He would then move around to different areas of the driveway and ask me again if I thought he could make it. My answer would always be the same no matter how far from the hoop he was or how difficult the shot. I believed in him and always tried to instill the confidence in him that he can make the shot regardless of how far he was from the hoop.

Your employees need to know that they can do something regardless of obstacles and time restraints. Henry Ford said, "Whether you think you can or can't, you're right." Send your subordinates in with positive fuel, and they will be more likely to succeed. Let them know that they have your support and confidence and that they can make the hoop regardless of how difficult the shot.

In a profession such as law enforcement, as I moved up in rank, it became more challenging to motivate as my position now was geared more toward daytime tasks, and police work is an around-the-clock profession. As a lieutenant overseeing sergeants, I had more day-to-day contact with the day-shift sergeants and less contact with the night-shift sergeants. I made sure to keep a calendar specifically for the nights that I planned on adjusting my schedule to work alongside the night supervisors which also allowed an opportunity to feel their subordinates' pulse. I would mark the dates that I made the night shift visits to assure that too many days did not pass without stopping by.

I would make sure to use this time to speak to all night-shift employees and answer any questions or even clear up inaccurate rumors which can spread very quickly when not controlled. I would also make sure to publicly praise performance and assure that even though I was not always around the night-shift squad, their supervisor would keep me abreast of what a great team they had. They would be visibly thrilled to know that their immediate supervisor was informing upper management of their great performance. For example, if an employee evaluation had recently crossed my desk, I would let that officer know that I read it and was very pleased with her or his performance and would ask that they keep up the great work and assure them that it does not go unnoticed.

In my evaluations to employees, I would take full advantage and use the evaluation as an additional tool to motivate them. I once had a sergeant under my supervision that was obviously the top performing and most dedicated sergeant of all. He had high expectations for his subordinates and truly motivated them to perform exceptional. It was evident that he took pride in his position as a leader, but for some reason, he would submit paperwork with more errors than any other sergeant. While I did not agree, I remember my father saying, "One oh shit erases all the at-a-boys." What he meant was that you can be a great employee, but if you mess up once, it will erase all the good you have done. Again, a phrase more suitable for different times. The paperwork errors kept me on my toes, but lucky for the sergeant, I did not adopt my dad's theory into my management style.

As I sat with this sergeant to review his annual evaluation with him, I used the opportunity to address the paperwork error issue. That was, of course, after I praised him for his excellent attributes and work ethics. I mean, he was truly an asset to the organization and definitely part of the team with the same positive vision and goals for the agency. I related his situation to one of the best basketball players of all times, Shaquille O'Neal. Shack was an amazing basketball player with a terrible free throw record of 52.7 percent. He had this one imperfection mixed in with his remarkable talent. But O'neal worked very hard on improving on his free throws and would try to make two hundred free throws a day at practice in attempt to improve his free throw percentage. He continued his superb performance in all other areas but focused on his deficiency and tried everything he could to improve in that area.

As I sat across from the sergeant administering him with his annual performance evaluation, I spoke to him about Shaquille O'Neal's one flaw. Fortunately, I did not let the paperwork errors be the sole basis for my evaluating the sergeant and harped mostly on his qualities. He seemed crushed in a way that I addressed the deficiency which further proved his dedication. I told him that it was not the end of the world and to be like Shack and focus hard on his area of shortcoming. I was very pleased to administer his next evaluation and praise him for the improvement in the area he once lacked in.

While many organizations utilize some sort of employee evaluation procedure, a supervisor shall never wait until the evaluation to praise an employee for great performance. Much of what is contained in an evaluation should be a review of what has already been addressed with an employee, shall it be praise or corrective measures. An evaluation should be considered a review of what has already been attended to.

One of my great officers had the opportunity to get promoted to sergeant after several years with the agency. While he was great at police work, I knew that there would be a transition period before he figured out that rather than being responsible for the job that we performed, he would now be responsible for the officers that performed the job functions. A great leader will realize that their customer will now not be their number one priority, the personnel that takes care of those customers is.

In speaking with the newly promoted sergeant, I tried to instill in him the idea of shifting his focus from performing his previous tasks to taking care of his team. One of the most important ways, I told him, was to make sure to never leave out praise and motivation. During our conversation, I also told him to always assess employees and try to catch them.

"Catch them?" he replied.

Knowing that he thought I was implying to catch employees messing up, I quickly replied "Yes, of course. Catch them doing something that merits praise." I added, "Use an opportunity as soon as possible to praise the employee, being detailed on why they are being praised." I made sure that he knew to never wait for a formal evaluation to outline the performances.

I further told the new sergeant to find out what motivates employees and to make sure to give them purpose. Lack of appreciation and recognition will lead to poor work production, and I advised him that this will usually be the leader's fault. I told him to master the art and know that not all employees are motivated the same way and that, sadly, some cannot be fully motivated at all.

One error that I have seen in managers and that I also experienced myself for some time was to expect others to possess the same motivation as I. If you are in a supervisory position at your place of employment or even just reading this book for self-improvement, you are already more motivated than most others within your organization. Having motivation and drive comes easier for some more than others. A great leader must know how to motivate someone that is different from them.

Never get disappointed when an employee's motivation begins to fade as a decrease in motivation is very common. How many people have you met that start a diet with extreme motivation and do not stick with it. Yea, just about everyone! This is the same reason that gyms are jam-packed in January and February and why they require you to sign a contract. If everyone's motivation always remained the same, there will be no need for a gym membership, and everyone would be walking around looking like Dwayne "The Rock" Johnson.

That is why when motivating, make sure to use the "staircase of motivation" approach. Picture your employee standing at the bottom of a staircase of motivation. Determine how high that employee is on the staircase when it comes to motivation. Some may be halfway up and others may not even have set foot on the first step. It is our job as leaders to get the employees to climb steps regardless of what step they are on.

As a leader in any organization, it should be a top priority to create different ways appropriate for each individual employee to motivate them to want to be at work and succeed at organizational tasks. As stated by the CEO of Whole Foods, John Mackey, "If you are lucky enough to be someone's employer, then you have a moral obligation to make sure people do look forward to coming to work in the morning." The main focus must be on the employees and their motivation, which can easily fade if not tended to.

I used to not even conceive how people could not be naturally motivated to perform exceptionally until eventually I realized that everyone is different and had different upbringings, goals, and motivators. As a supervisor, I would get frustrated at the fact that my subordinates were not at my level until one day I began to utilize the staircase of motivation philosophy. As where before I would think that there was no hope for certain employees because of their lack of drive, I changed my technique and geared my motivational system into attempting to get that employee to a higher step on the staircase, rather than at the top step were I was.

There are a few simple steps to motivation. One important step is to create a pleasant work environment. A grumpy boss equals a decrease in production and toxic work culture. No one enjoys working in a negative work environment; therefore, a boss must stride to create a positive work environment. A positive environment includes a favorable work area for employees to perform their duties. It also includes interacting with employees and praising them rather than scolding. Rewards and recognition goes a long way, and it will be the topic of discussion later that night at the dinner table. If this becomes the norm, when the time comes to address a deficiency, the employee will take the constructive criticism easier and respect that you are addressing it.

The old phrase "Praise in public, discipline in private" is still valid today, and public praise should never be left out. In group meetings with employees, at least one employee, if not more, should be publicly praised about a particular incident.

Purpose

Motivation should drive a feeling of purpose. Purpose-driven employees are more likely to perform at a higher level. While employed at the telecommunications company, the owner, Keith, constantly reminded me of my value and made it clear of my purpose in the organization. I felt valued, and in return, my work performance level was always elevated. Without a sense of purpose, employees are sure to get in a rut, which will lower drive and result in poorer performance.

We all need a purpose. My middle son, Ryan, was a member of the Boy Scouts as well as the Civil Air Patrol (CAP). When attending his weekly meetings with him, I always noticed that there were always adult volunteers. It soon came to me that these adult members, most of them parents as well, wanted to have a purpose and some responsibilities in the platoon members and their activities. It gave them the purpose that is similar to what our employees need to feel.

Purpose gives direction and gives a reason for existence. It gives employees a sense of meaning in the organization. It becomes difficult to motivate an employee with no sense of purpose. A leader must find out an employee's purpose and align their persuasive efforts with them in order to better motivate.

Motivate Yourself

As a leader, you know that your key task is motivating your team. You are constantly creating ways to keep them motivated to successfully complete organizational tasks and feel good about coming to work. But how does a leader stay motivated themselves? Many leaders are primarily motivated by accomplishing leadership goals. In addition to achieving goals, leaders must continuously come up with ways to stay motivated themselves.

A leader that is truly self-motivated will not have an issue coming up with ways to stay driven. True leaders always want more for themselves and set goals to keep themselves motivated. Being innovative and advancing the organization is one way to stay motivated. I spoke earlier about having a true aspiration to make positive changes in your organization, and a great leader will set organizational goals to meet. Setting organizational goals can keep a leader motivated to achieve them.

Furthermore, leaders must be an alumni of the leadership community and look for role models to follow. Reading books, attending seminars, and staying informed of current leadership blogs should be a common practice for a leader. Staying informed on current leadership trends will keep you sharp in your delivery at your organization. Motivation comes from constant learning to be better, which will bring you more confidence in your duties. But motivating yourself is not solely reliant on reading books, rather challenging yourself in whatever ways possible to flourish your leadership development.

While at the dinner table one evening discussing a prepaid college plan for our children, one of our little ones asked what we were talking about. I explained how a college plan works to them and followed it up with a stern, "So you, guys, better go to college!" One of them innocently replied by asking me if I went to college. Sadly, I had not been to college at this point other than a police academy that was located on a college campus. That was the moment that I decided to register and begin my academic journey.

While my children were the main focus of getting my college degree, I became self-motivated to complete the program not only for my kids but so that my parents can be proud of their son, the college graduate. The motivation to get my degree continued on from an associate's degree to a bachelor's degree and then a master's degree and on up. Until one day, I sat with my children and read my acceptance letter for my Doctor of Philosophy degree to them. It began with a small push from my kids but continued with a self-motivation to accomplish the ultimate degree.

While not every leader aspires to obtain a PhD, they must always figure out ways to set a good example to others. My motivation began with setting a good example to my kids and blossomed into setting a good example to coworkers. Throughout the years, employees looked to me for guidance on obtaining their degrees, and I was fortunate to guide them in the right direction. Motivating employees to achieve their educational goals was motivating to me but could not have happened without my desire to self-develop.

One must constantly look for challenges to develop their talents and seek virtues in their lives. Reviewing your past accomplishments and setting goals for future ones will keep you motivated. In doing so, you will inspire people and become a mentor in the lives of others which will benefit you as a leader and result in self-motivation. When a leader stays on track with their self-development, they will build a solid foundation to their success, which will in itself produce motivation.

Chapter Eight

Problem and Conflict Solving

In many organizations, your value depends on how well your problem and conflict solving skills are. In addition to motivating employees and addressing organizational issues, leaders are constantly solving problems, and it should be embraced as part of your duties. Employees should feel confident in bringing problems and concerns to you and know that you will assist them in resolving them. Colin Powell said, "The day the soldiers stop bringing you their problems is the day you stopped leading them. They have either lost confidence that you can help them or conclude that you do not care. Either case is a failure of leadership."

One of the essential leadership tasks is to minimize the occurrences of problems and conflicts. A true leader is courageous enough to tackle issues of concern related to obstructions that will hinder organizational progress or morale. Whether faced with a problem that needs to be solved or a conflict that needs to be addressed, the leader must create a solid strategy and map out a plan of action to address it.

Problem Solving

There will be some employees that are problem solvers themselves and are usually the ones that move up quickly to supervisory positions. During my days as an operations manager at the telecommunications company, there were times that I would roll up on a project in the field and meet with the project manager for an update on the progress of a project. I was always impressed when I was briefed on the project and explained about a certain problem that was encountered immediately followed by what was done to overcome the hindrance.

The problem encountered was addressed and overcome by the team figuring out what to do without ever calling me. That is not to say that they couldn't have called me if they needed to. The project manager added value to himself by problem solving rather than quickly calling me when he encountered it. He took initiative, as a leader should, and successfully overcame an obstacle. I would have also been just as satisfied if he would have contacted me and said, "I tried A and B, but it didn't seem to work. Can you suggest what we can do to conquer this?"

At the telecommunications company, the owner, Keith Manalio, approached me one afternoon and said, "Fred, I have a problem!"

Without hesitating, I replied, "Let's find a solution!"

The problem would hinder the company from making a good deal of money on a new project. A major cable TV company was in the beginning stages of replacing all underground cables with cable-in-conduit (CIC) and was offering us a major part of the project. Keith knew that given the desired projected time of completion for the project, we would not be able to take on too much being that we were not sufficiently staffed for the project and that several hundreds of thousands of dollars in equipment will need to be purchased to complete it. If we were not able to commit to all of it, another company would have been brought in to share the project or even worse outbid us and take the whole thing.

During this time in the mid-'90s, the World Wide Web was not yet booming as it is today, but the vice president, Ed Rose, had provided me with a unfamiliar device that I was slowly getting better acquainted with. I told Keith to give me a couple of days to figure something out. In doing some research on my new computer thingy, I found a website where traveling contractors offered their services and were able to bid for available jobs. After making several contacts and putting out descriptive details about the project, I was able to hire some out-of-state contractors willing to travel and assist with the job. I ran it by Keith, of course, and told him to take on the project.

The following Monday morning, when Keith arrived to work, there were around a dozen work trucks with equipment trailers attached parked down the street and more than a few workers standing outside of the trucks waiting to get to work. Keith's face was priceless, and he couldn't believe how fast I was able to man the project with zero equipment cost. Needless to say, there were hefty Christmas bonuses that year, and most importantly, I added value to myself by solving the problem.

Conflict Solving

There is a great chance that in just about every organization, there are a few employees that will not be satisfied with anything you have to offer. They are interweaved within your personnel and somehow have meddled into your work establishment. These particular employees may fall into the 25 percent that cannot be swayed aboard or the 50 percent that can be swayed to either side. Regardless, they need not be ignored. They need to be gently and progressively persuaded aboard the motivation bus. Totally ignoring their problems can result in them gradually pulling others off the bus with them. Many leaders will try getting away with "waiting and seeing" if the problem works itself out. If their actions are toxic, it needs to be addressed immediately.

When I was the operations manager at KM Contracting Inc., the field installers were issued a work route in a particular area. We covered a large tri-county area, and most installers preferred certain areas of which I would attempt to satisfy their requests with. There was, of course, a few employees that constantly complained about an assigned area and when moved to their desired area would find something else to complain about. An experienced leader knows that unfortunately these employees will usually exist and will create individual tactics to address their constant concerns.

A fine line should always be drawn when attempting to satisfy employees as to not cater to their every need when they receive their assignments. The fact will become present that some employees will nearly always have a negative concern. The goal is to put the square peg in the square hole and the round peg in the round hole when appointing assignment. Eventually, with some care and attention by the leader, for a majority of employees, the satisfaction chips will fall into place. For the ones that will not respond to anything, they are not to be totally given up on, but most of your efforts should not be given to them, rather to the more responsive ones that you can get to the next step on the staircase.

In police work, a union usually negotiates a contract for the officers around every four years. For some reason, there is always build-up just before a contract negotiation, and a rumor will spread like a wildfire on the extravagant raises that are to come. The optimism drives all employees to begin to make plans with the money to come, which usually leads to disappointment. Although the police agency that

I worked for saw consistent raises every year, everyone was not always satisfied with the outcome of the contract. Many employees were grateful for the raise, but for several weeks after the final contract, there were some fires that needed to be put out. For most employees, fires were put out, and they eventually learned to live with the outcome. For others, the fire will occasionally spark back up, and their fire needed a new dose of water.

One day, an officer's fire lit back up on the topic of money, and he requested to speak to me about the subject. While deep down inside it was a broken record that I had heard him play many times, I worked through it and listened attentively. I tried my best to come up with a verbal resolution that will put him somewhat at ease by speaking of what we have and not what we should have. I spoke to him about how fortunate we are to have a rewarding profession and how much more we now have since prior to our employment with the organization. The officer was visibly troubled, and while it was my sole mission at the moment, I could not get him even near where I was trying to get him. There was an obvious underlying issue present in his demeanor, and the outcome was not the one I was going for.

The officer got up and told me that I was not understanding him and he didn't wish to discuss it any further. He stormed out of my office, unsatisfied with the meeting, and I remained puzzled at what exactly it was that he was trying to get out of the meeting. Was he trying to drag me down to his level so that I agreed with him on his concerns, or was there something that I could have done to resolve his problem?

Later that evening, I sat at home pondering his true reason for bringing his problem to me. I determined that he was all out of complaints and decided to revisit an issue that was of previous concern to him. Unfortunately, this was a problem that was out of my hands to solve as it was a contractual and out of my power to change. It was then that I realized that despite leaders being problem solvers, his problem was not one that needed solving. Instead, his issue required active listening with positive feedback. The idea was outlined in a book by Barry Johnson called *Polarity Management* which states that sometimes you're going to come up against something that's not a problem to be solved but a tension to be managed. This particular employee's tension needed management, and I was trying my best to solve it as if it were a problem.

Some supervisors will avoid problems and conflict at all cost. During my early age as a police officer, when negativity existed in disgruntled employees, there were a few sergeants that did not embrace problems or conflict as part of their duties. I distinctly remember a sergeant being asked by a former lieutenant to address an issue with one of his officers, and his reply to the lieutenant was, "I'm not losing any more friends!" He blatantly refused to address the issue which in turn developed into something much worse.

I later came to the realization that the lieutenant should have properly guided the sergeant and advised him to embrace the idea that addressing an issue of concern can be productive if managed constructively. In this case, the sergeant was not the sole member at fault for not performing his duty to address an issue. The lieutenant also failed to intervene on the sergeant's inability or non-desire to act which unfortunately later reached a level of intractability.

Chapter Nine

Leading Up

There is more than one definition to the word leader. In addition to the many definitions of a leader, some state that a leader is a person in charge of a group, and others read that a leader motivates a group toward a common goal. A successful organization consists of the efforts of every employee from the CEO down. If you are in a leadership position but also have a boss to respond to, you will need to realize that both your boss and subordinates have their own goals and needs, and you must lead them both accordingly.

Holding any leadership rank does not necessarily mean that you are required only to lead the personnel under your command. If leadership includes influencing others in an organization, then it is important that you also include the personnel that hold a higher rank than you into your leading practices. We must be a leader to our leaders. I'll explain.

Early in my career as a sergeant, the agency had a cutback in training, and when training was available, the officers were sent to an outside entity to participate in the training events, being that we were a smaller agency and did not have a training center. I knew that there were several police-related trainings that we should have been performing in-house together as a team. When the feces hits the fan in my profession, it is important that your fellow officers have trained together and know each other's tactics. I thought it would be a good idea to propose that we perform certain trainings internally, and I even offered to take lead on some of the subjects.

I was mostly motivated to put together internal training events because I remember as an officer hearing other employees constantly complaining about how we needed more training. How better to boost morale and employee bonding than to train together and get out of the daily routine for a while, which was something that was not common in our organization at the time. I had a precognition that the request was going to get denied, and that's exactly what happened. Several reasons were given to me as to why we could not perform the trainings internally. This suggestion being turned down taught me a valuable lesson. It taught me that when you come to someone with a problem, be ready to give a suggested solution. It also taught me that if at first you don't succeed, dust yourself off and try again.

The course that I was presenting was an active shooter training. Since the unfortunate school shooting at Columbine High School in 1999, there have been several others that followed, causing law enforcement to now have enough reliable data to create tactics on how to respond to such tragedies. The suggested training was way before active shootings became a hot topic; therefore, it was easier for the chief at the time to deny it. Given the current times, I would hope that he would have approved it, but back then, the agency was in a state of stagnation, and that is why I was trying so hard to put it together.

I also figured it would be a fun course to where we can, together as a group, run through the drills and tactics and break from the normal daily routines. I came up with a new idea before I re-presented it. I created a lesson plan and PowerPoint presentation and contacted Miami Airsoft, a local airsoft company that agreed to allow us to use their equipment for the training. They even offered to provide role players for the event, which made it that much more realistic. I also made suggested changes to the work schedule so that officers can attend without impacting the daily operations of the agency. Oh, and by the way, I made sure that no overtime would be incurred by the event.

Fortunately, with all the legwork and planning already completed by me, the training event was approved. It was a huge hit! Officers came together and completed active scenarios and enjoyed working together. The most senior officer in the organization even wrote an official memorandum to the chief of police, expressing his appreciation for me creating a training event that we performed together internally.

It was extremely rewarding to sit back quietly immediately after the training event and watch the members of our organization full of energy and laughing while they conversed about the scenarios that were performed during the event.

The chief at the time, who should have probably read this book, began to gloat about how we are moving in a new direction, and we were now going to conduct several trainings internally. I had no problem with the chief taking credit for the change. I was most of all excited that I was able to bring something new to the organization that boosted morale and teamwork.

I was only at the rank of sergeant that by definition said that I lead officers, but in this case, I had just lead the chief of police and made him look good. That's no different than leading the personnel under you. If they look good, you look good, so why not pass the credit up too. The agency would eventually create a training unit, and in addition to the external trainings, dozens were performed internally, and we became that much better because of it.

In the case of leading up, you must bring valuableness to the table and perform as if you were already in a higher position. This trait must be performed tactfully so that you don't step on any boss's toes and know your place within the organization. A rule of thumb is to run the organization as if you were the owner, this way your performance and decisions will never make the CEO look bad.

True leadership is more than only touching the employees under your command. Employees need to be part of organizational changes and cultivating buy-in from higher-ranking personnel within an agency, which should be seen as an important task for middle managers. An important factor in leadership is standing up for issues and pointing out a better way to the bosses. Successfully implementing a change works best when members at every level agree with a favorable resolution. If you can acquire the magical skill of persuading the boss into a decision, then you are on track to leading her or him as well as your subordinates.

Actions are contagious. Negative people usually turn people around them negative too, and positive people will usually be surrounded by other positive people. Great leadership alike can be contagious, and when your supervisor sees your great leadership qualities, they, too, will mimic your performance. You may have a boss that has been in the business for several years whose leadership qualities have not purposely slowly diminished. When you are able to infect your boss with positive and effective leadership qualities that they perform because of your actions, then you are successfully leading up.

So as a leader, if you are not at the top chain of command, you have a responsibility to influence your boss while overseeing the operations of the organization. A lot of times we get so caught up in the day-to-day issues of leading our team that we forget how important it is to lead up the chain and building a strong relationship with our boss. In many instances, your boss can be an angel or the devil himself. The first step in getting in good with the boss is to effectively communicate with them.

Many leaders are dominant-minded and forget that their boss is the one that is actually in charge. Actively listening to your supervisor and refraining from talking over her or him is very important. There is an art to communication, and while listening, try to pick up on some of the things that the boss is not saying. What is not said can later be brought up by you as a suggestion. It is okay to tell the boss that she or he just gave you a great idea. When explaining the idea, make sure to ask them what they think about the idea. You will not be less of a great leader if the idea is implemented, and you give the boss full credit for the idea.

For some leaders, the biggest problem they have is not properly leading their team, rather dealing with the issues pertaining to their boss. It is easier to get feedback from your team members and collectively come up with a decision for implementation than convincing your boss of something to be executed. Ultimately, the decision lies on the person with the most power similar to a parent making the final decision at home. Some kids have become the master of influencing their parents to allow them to do something without any formal training on how to do so. They have just used what they know will work.

Sometimes, people are put in a management position to make organizational changes, which can take up to a few months to do. During the time that you are working on making effective adjustments to the company, you should be attempting to decode the boss's train of thinking. You should make your style blend in with theirs so that effective influencing can occur without taking away from the boss's authority. Remember, to your boss, you are first seen as an investment before you are seen as a value to the organization. Focus on the task at hand, the personnel under your command, and definitely the needs of your superior.

Chapter Ten

Recognition, Praise, and Appreciation

Undoubtedly, it's a good idea for supervisors to get into the habit of regularly recognizing performance and letting employees know that they are appreciated. As stated by John Adair, "Praise and recognition based upon performance are the oxygen of the human spirit." Recognition, praise, and appreciation can increase work production if administered properly. They are all three important but somewhat different from each other.

Recognition should focus on what the employee does, and appreciation is more about what kind of person the employee is. Praise is geared more toward admiration and approval. It is imperative that employees receive all three from their supervisor. Some employees, unfortunately, perform well and do not receive any of the three, but when they make a mistake, it seems like they never hear the end of it. In the words of Dale Carnegie, "Once I did bad, and that I heard ever. Twice I did good, but that I heard never."

Recognition

The need for recognition is paramount. I once took a weekend getaway trip to Washington, DC, with my wife to enjoy some alone time visiting our great US capital. We enjoyed our time there, visiting all the historic sites, but unfortunately our alone time had ran out, and it was time to head back home. We boarded the plane and made our way to our assigned seats which happened to be directly behind a young mother holding a newborn baby. Having four children of our own, the fact that the baby would be sure to cry sometime during the flight did not bother us at all.

To our surprise, we did not hear a peep from the newborn. We watched that just as the plane began to take off, the mother draped a nursing shawl over her and began to breastfeed the baby. Within seconds, the baby was fast asleep, and the mom laid the baby down in the seat next to her, already made up with a cozy quilt. It was as if she had timed the feeding perfectly for takeoff time. Sometime later, the baby woke up, and the mom already had a toy in hand ready to entertain the baby. Once the baby began to lose interest in the toy, the mom pulled a children's book from her bag and instantly transitioned from the toy to the book. My wife and I watched through the crack of the seat in front of us and couldn't help to analyze her perfect orchestration for keeping the baby entertained and quiet on the plane ride.

When the plane landed at our destination, I heard someone say to the young mother, "What a well-behaved baby you have! I couldn't even tell there was a newborn on the flight."

My wife and I giggled since we had witnessed that it was actually the mother that was responsible for the baby's behavior. Unfortunately, the mom did not get recognized for the things she had done to keep the baby quiet during the plane ride. Not that she needed the recognition in this situation, I'm sure, but what employees do at work does need recognition in order for the desired actions to be repeated. An employee's work product should be recognized as performed by them, just as the young mother's actions resulted in the favorable behavior of the newborn on the plane.

There are several ways to recognize employee performance. Recognition should not be confused with praise, appreciation, or even motivation, though recognizing performance is somewhat related to those three in one way or another. Recognition can be taken as praise and appreciation and may even motivate some to continue favorable performance. Regardless, recognition must be incorporated into every organization that depends on employees to operate. It can be administered in a variety of ways.

It can be issued in ways such as awards, extra time off, and giving "props" to an employee for a job well done. Many organizations look at production numbers and attendance when making a decision on who to administer recognition to. That is one way to recognize, but leaders should be on the lookout for other actions that merit recognition. All organizations should have a policy that outlines forms of recognition to employees. If yours does not, you as a leader must create one to be implemented immediately.

At the telecommunications company that I worked for, we award the technicians with the highest percentage of completed jobs with a gift certificate. These were employees that had the lowest number of job cancellations or reschedules. It was a small incentive for having high numbers. Similarly, the technicians whose jobs passed all quality control inspections for the month earned eight hours of paid time off (PTO), which will allow them to take a paid day off. This incentive was a big hit that the employees always strived to achieve. It also was a good tool to keep them performing quality work.

The police department also has several forms of recognitions in place, such as officer of the month and officer of the year. It is important though when making a decision on who to nominate with such awards to make it legitimate and never base your decision on a single event. The decision to recognize should be on a total accumulation of all performance. Unfairly awarding an employee of the month or year can cause tension within the organization and possibly decrease motivation in others.

Some organizations give bonuses as recognition for high performance, such as sales, which can motivate employees to hit the desired numbers. This sort of reward recognition must be done carefully as it can set employees against one another, leading to conflict. Although some say that money should not be a motivator, all employees have monetary needs that can give a sense of security when fulfilled. Recognition in the form of money should never be the primary motivator for favorable performance, rather another tool in your recognition toolbox.

Praise

Praise is the expression of gratefulness and should be specific. Merely saying "Good job today" at the end of a shift seems meaningless and does not specifically identify what is being praised. When praising, it is important to be event specific, such as saying "It is amazing how you always guide employees and get them up to speed" or "It's nice to see how you always keep your composure when the going gets tough."

Many "bosses" will conduct management by walking around and say "Good job" to just about everyone they encounter. When you hear it said to just about everyone, it devalues the phrase and becomes meaningless. It is more effective to pinpoint a specific event and harp on it in detail, praising the action. For example, "I overheard you dealing with that complaint today. I was really impressed with the way you handled it." Praising in detail will have the best effect and will motivate the employee to repeat the performance. When you get into a habit of praising, it will become second nature when an incidents that merits praise is identified and you will praise without even thinking about it.

Unfortunately, it seems that longevity is no longer as common in the workplace as it was decades ago. It is less common to see someone stay with one organization for thirty or forty years, and job-hopping appears to be on the rise. According to a survey conducted by CareerBuilder, 50 percent of employees said they believed turnover would decrease if managers simply recognized their efforts more frequently. As previously indicated, a supervisor shall never wait for a formal evaluation to praise an employee and shall administer it frequently. A turnover rate within an agency should never be a result of lack of praise.

Appreciation

Everyone wants to feel appreciated whether it is at work by supervisors and coworkers or at home by our spouses. Just as in a marriage, one should not assume that our subordinates know that we appreciate them. Like praise, appreciation should be continuously expressed. Expressing appreciation will make an employee feel that their work is valued. Appreciating someone makes them feel good about what they do, and in doing so, they are likely to repeat such performance.

Appreciation is much like praise and can be administered in different ways. A handwritten note or e-mail telling someone you appreciate them goes a long way in the workplace. I once walked into the office of our emergency management coordinator and saw a framed e-mail from our captain to him stating encouraging words of appreciation. It was obviously important enough to him to frame it and display it in his office. Similarly, a public service aide once gave me a handwritten Christmas card with words of appreciation so meaningful to me that I still have displayed in my office today.

Asking an employee if there is anything you can do to help will also go a long way. Occasionally, you can show appreciation by stepping in and assisting with a task. A good leader should be well-rounded in all the functions within an organization and stepping in, and getting her or his hands dirty will keep them sharp in the tasks performed. When a supervisor steps in to help, it will create a sense of comradery between the employee and the supervisor and provide an appreciation for what they do.

Not recognizing, praising, or appreciating employees can have a harmful effect on morale and production. The appreciation must be genuine, though. It is not a good idea to fake appreciation as it can undermine the employee relationship. When there is no performance present that merits recognition, praise, or appreciation, then your focus should become more on motivating. When an employee rises higher on the staircase of motivation, then incidents that merit the recognitions and praise will begin to appear.

Chapter Eleven

Custom Leadership

Holding a supervisory role in any organization holds a difficult task just in the fact that various age groups may be present and employees may be at different stages in their career. Keeping that in mind, your supervisory styles may need to be customized depending on employee age groups and tenure within the organization. I cannot emphasize enough that a one-size-fits-all leadership style will not work in a multigenerational workplace.

I once attended a middle management class in college, and during the professor's opening statements to the class, he was comparing managers to leaders and asked the class if they thought leaders were born or made. Though I really didn't want to be the first to answer, I also did not want to contradict anyone in the class that may have answered before me, so I raised my hand. When called on by the professor, I answered that I thought everyone is born with a leadership quality that can be developed; therefore, I believe leaders are made. He had obviously asked this question to other classes before, but he gave me an interested look and said, "Can you explain further, please?"

I continued by telling him that leaders are lifelong learners, and when you throw various generation into the equation, there is a learning and adaptation process for the leader that I believed can translate as "made." I continued by adding that his question may have been around for many centuries and could have been answered ages ago by saying that leaders are born. Back in the days, before a mixture of baby boomers, Generation Zs, and millennials, saying that leaders were born would have probably been a correct answer, but the path that the world has taken now requires leaders to continuously learn the ways of the generations and what works when leading them.

I believe my answer was one that the professor may not have heard before, and while he never really admitted it, I believe that the professor has always leaned more toward born than made. Other students would later chime into the debate and give some interesting but true answers to his question. Nevertheless, the question sparked up an interactive participation in the conversation by all the student in attendance.

I can remember when the year 2000 seemed like an eternity away and when we were certain that by 2020, the sky would be filled with flying cars. While technology has greatly advanced during the twenty-first century, the workforce has always possessed employees of different generations. So, wrap your head around this! Some employees under your supervision may have not even been born during the attacks of September 11, 2001, and others may remember it as if it were yesterday. We're talking about people who were in their twenties or thirties before the smartphone was invented and others that do not even know what a dial tone is, all under one roof and under your wing.

Mike and the Mechanics sing a song that says, "Every generation, blames the one before." It is far too common to see this mentality in the workplace. It is also common for an older generation to criticize a younger generation's ways and vice versa. A true leader will recognize that there is nothing particularly "wrong" with a specific generation. There ways are normal to them, considering the times and what they are accustomed to. It is the leader that must recognize what actions produce successful outcomes, and we must flourish them with a results mechanism.

At the police department, we actually had very young newly hired police officers that could not get around the city without a GPS device and for the life of them were unable to identify which way north was. As you can imagine, geography is critical in law enforcement, and time is of the essence when responding to an emergency situation. There is obviously no time to punch an address into a GPS. The simple task of locating addresses created a whole new approach for the field training officers when it came to training the technologically infused demographic.

I actually once saw a young employee taking a photo with his cellular phone of some paperwork that he had handwritten prior to turning it in. To my surprise, when I asked him why he was taking the photo, he told me that he is able to better proofread it from his phone than by looking directly on the paper. While I was internally shocked and thought that this was strangely bizarre, prior to making him feel bad about his technique, it dawned on me that I am actually the opposite. I can proofread a loose leaf document easier than a document on an electronic device. Fortunately, I kept my composure and simply replied, "Whatever works!"

Conversely, upon implementing a new idea to the troops one day, I went around the room and asked for feedback and suggestions. The change would mostly affect them; therefore, I wanted to get a feel for how they felt about it prior to implementation. Not surprisingly, the baby boomers did not provide much feedback while the millennials could not stop throwing feedback and suggestions at me. Later in the day, I met with a one of the senior employees alone and asked how he felt about the previously discussed idea. He shrugged his shoulders and said, "Its fine." I giggled politely and recreated the question by asking if he had any suggestions to it. He did not, but I made sure to ask him that if he had thought of anything throughout the day to please let me know.

As previously stated, employees from different generations cannot perform under a one-size-fits-all method. Millennials, for example, may need to be occasionally assigned different projects while baby boomers may be set in their ways and feel overwhelmed with various assignments. A good manager will get a feel for their staff and place them where appropriate. The assignments and tasks performed, of course, must benefit the organization as well. This task may take some meaningful communicating with the employees and may take some time to figure out.

Undoubtedly, one thing that is common in all generations is that no matter one's age or tenure, all employees need to have a personal sense of meaning in the organization. They need to be treated with respect and feel a sense of purpose. Purpose will help drive them toward a satisfying future with the organization. Their purpose would be the reason they get up in the morning and go to work.

Ultimately, a leader in any organization must learn the ways of all generations present. With various management styles, such as autocratic, democratic, and laissez-faire, anyone that identifies with only one will be less successful at certain aspects of leadership. Similarly, a leader that identifies with only one generation's ways will only impact a portion of the organization's members, making it partially successful. One must always work on becoming a well-rounded leader that positively impacts all members.

It will be a mistake to stereotype one particular generation and expect that they will respond to a particular leadership style simply because of their age. There are many individuals though that perform to a level opposite of their era norms. Some baby boomers may adapt to current times, and some millennials may have an old soul way of doing things. It is important for leaders to observe employees and use a tactic appropriate for each individual employee.

I have been the head of several trainings throughout the years, and when it comes to police training events, there are always several questions about how to perform a certain task, especially in a tactical situation. The appropriate answer is usually that the situation will dictate what the response will be since every situation is different. The same goes for leading different generations. Everyone is different, and while you can generally supervise a certain generation a particular way, it should never be a one-size-fits-all approach. Customizing your leadership is the only way to get the desired outcome from employees.

Improve by Changing

Great leaders must be adaptable and open to changing themselves. The least successful leaders are the ones that are set in their ways and believe that an "old school" way is the only way. I have had to adapt to many things over the years in my personal and business life. When my kids told me that they were allowed to take their cellular phones to school, I had to verify that it was true. I mean even the United States military allows you to bring one to basic training. These are things that seem unconceivable to some but are the norm to the newer generation.

The best leaders learn from others and have the ability to pivot from generation to generation, leading employees the way that works for them. Because change is constant, a leader must learn to adapt in order to succeed. I remember when Myspace users would not get a Facebook account if you paid them. Then everyone had Facebook, and all those same users would then say "No way!" to Instagram. Many are reluctant to change and remain set in their ways, but a leader cannot afford to live by those rules.

I spoke earlier about being a change agent and how it is important to not remain stagnant in your leadership style. This not only includes creating change but accepting the modernistic changes that have come and are yet to come. Leaders that respond to change suggestions by saying "We are doing okay without it" or "We are not ready for that" can hold the organization many steps behind. The ones that are able to customize their leadership to a given time are the ones that successfully identify new priorities and fit them together with the needs of organizational progress.

Chapter Twelve

Leading during a Crisis

In a leadership position, we are held with the responsibility of making decisions that can affect dozens, hundreds, or even thousands of people in many cases. In some professions, a wrong decision made by a leaders can mean life or death. Leadership, in part, involves persuading employees to collectively be responsible for the outcomes of the work performed. If you wrap your head around that for a moment, you will realize how important decision-making is for a leader. Now imagine the intensity of your decisions when making them during a time of crisis.

On September 11, 2001, Islamic extremists hijacked planes and carried out attacks against targets in the United Stated. The events on that day undoubtedly changed history forever. Although the actions of great leaders helped reshape the recovery of our country during those events, most of their decisions and actions did not make the headlines.

While being tasks with a quick recovery, New York City Mayor Rudolph Giuliani and former President George W. Bush were not the only leaders to make it happen. Many leaders on the ground had to be responsible for rescue and recovery workers that were dealing not only with the task at hand but with the thought of over 2,600 people that lost their lives including more than four hundred firefighters and police officers as a result of the attacks. Leaders on the grounds of the World Trade Center that day and during the days after performed amazing tasks, and informal leaders took the bulls by the horns and performed leadership decisions that saved lives.

In the early months of 2020, the infectious disease, coronavirus (COVID-19), made its way around the world, affecting the ways of life for everyone. As many were ordered to stay home during this time to prevent the spread of the virus, police officers and other first responders were going to work and asked to perform their duties very differently than they were used to. It was definitely a time for leaders to step up and take the actions necessary to protect their employees so that they can properly serve their communities.

Being located in South Florida, having our world shaken up was nothing new to us as we were directly in the path of several hurricanes during hurricane seasons and received near direct and direct hits several times. But COVID-19 was very different than hurricanes. With hurricanes, we took shelter, and when the storm passed and it was safe enough to come outside, we would assess and execute a pre-written plan for recovery. With COVID-19, we were battling an invisible opponent that changed the way policing was performed. The leaders of our organization now had to create policies and procedures that were not in place and outfit officers with personal protection equipment that was quickly becoming unavailable because of high demands.

Many procedures were created to keep our staff safe, such as how we now responded to calls. And what were we to do if COVID-19 spread through the department, infecting every officer? It was not as if we could have a neighboring police agency to assist us as they were also combating their own battle and would surely not be able to assist. As the leaders of the organization, we always had a responsibility to protect our people, but with this new and unexpected infection threatening our community, our responsibilities intensified.

Our employees knew that they swore an oath and would still have to come to work and perform to the best of their abilities. That didn't change the fact that they were worried and had several question for us regarding the way they were to perform their tasks now. Our main responsibilities now as leaders was to create policies and procedures and properly guide our employees and make them feel as safe as we possibly could considering the circumstances.

Several police officers from other agencies had already fallen victim to COVID-19, and while police officers have a hard time showing their emotions, you could feel the eeriness within the organization. First responders where once again put to the test and again hailed as heroes. For first responders, it was always a roller coaster of emotions of whether we were loved or hated depending on what was trending in the media at the moment. We had not been truly appreciated for a long time the way we were in September 2001.

Despite receiving warm appreciation from the people we served during the COVID-19 pandemic, there were constant changes occurring. There were even daily changes as new, and updated information was given regarding the infection. That alone can be a challenge for your frontline personnel during a crisis; therefore, it is a must that as a leader, you communicate constantly with your personnel. Crisis management requires honest communication and staying in touch with your employees on what is happening. Whether it is changing procedure because of newly obtained information or even bad news regarding a situation, keeping people informed quickly will assist in trust building. Leaders that hold back information during these times will quickly lose the trust of the troops.

It has been said that a leader's strengths are revealed during a time of pressure and difficulties. Employees admire leaders that can deal with tough incidents at the onset of the issue and show confidence that a clear decision is being made. Showing leadership confidence and staying positive during times of stress and anxiety will be imitated by subordinates and summon the mentality needed to maximize employee contributions. Some incidents will require leaders to guide personnel newly assigned to them, but in most occurrences, the people under their supervision are the ones that have been with them prior to the crisis striking.

But the COVID-19 pandemic affected some of the ways we commonly lead as it pertains to connecting with employees. Social distancing became a new hindrance to engaging with employees. A handshake or hug became forbidden as the attempt to stop the spread occurred. Needless to say, there was not much contact, and some employees were even forced to stay home. During this unprecedented time, it became evident that our employees' well-being was one of the most important issues that affected our organization.

Many "nonessential" personnel were forced to work from home, and while we now had a greater responsibility as a police agency, we made sure not to forget to check on our staff away at home. While the situation was troubling to all, it became another opportunity to demonstrate empathy and showcase our care for them. Simple out-of-the-blue phone calls to check on them proved valuable during the pandemic. And if we were able to send a care package from time to time, it only strengthened the connection with them. The objective of staying in contact with them, keeping them feeling important, and providing needed supplies to them as needed was to make them feel as essential as can be given that they were unfortunately now labeled "nonessential." A label that I really did not like much.

Whether a hurricane, terrorist attack, or deadly infectious disease pandemic, leaders are looked upon for information, guidance, hope, and encouragement. The tasks normally performed will greatly change during crisis, but this will not be the time to begin to prove yourself as leaders to your employees. All the aspects discussed in this book should have been occurring way before you lead through an unexpected crisis. Building trust must occur from day one, and if unfortunately a crisis hits, employees will be prepared to follow you into any battle.

I had to explain this to my brother once at a get together that I attended at his house. I somehow got into a conversation with a friend of his, Alex, about leadership at the get together. Alex and I had a lot in common as he was in a leadership position in the hospitality business. Alex had also read several of the same books as I and follows the same motivational speakers. He was obviously a student of the game at his profession, and I truly was enjoying our conversation. After about one hour into the discussion, my brother butted in and said, "Okay! Let's say we were about to go into battle and you had to motivate me. What would you say?"

I explained to my brother that while there were several onetime motivating speeches that could be given, the great traits of leadership occur during a long period of time. I told him that with time working together, he would have built trust in me as a leader, and regardless of what I said prior to heading into battle, he would have been ready to follow me into whatever the mission was. While it is not impossible to begin to be seen as a good leader at a time of crisis, having a head start as a result of your previous attributes will place you several steps ahead when the unimaginable occurs.

Since time is usually of the essence during a crisis, it is best when a leader takes a proactive approach when making decisions. Confident planning on the part of the leader can result in a calm feeling of security in the subordinates. Leadership styles may need to be altered during a crisis, and subordinates may be fixated on a particular leadership style. It is okay to create a new starting line with your people and explain that new goals are present considering crisis circumstances that may be present.

You may not always be ready for the crisis that you and your team are faced with. We were definitely not prepared for COVID-19, but preparations were made within our organization in advance to train a team ready and willing to fight any battle as a result of the environment that had been created long before the pandemic occurred. Many times, the crisis itself does not make the organization stumble, rather the leadership in place that causes the most destruction.

Ultimately, when leading during a crisis, the focus should be on the greater goal. A leader's mission must be aligned with his message. Part of the leader's mission is to get people on board with what the organization needs and what needs to be done to get it there. How you communicate your message will have the greatest result on how you lead. I have heard bosses too many times say, "No news is good news." When no information disseminating is a good thing, the organization may be in big trouble.

In addition to communication, there has to be a concern for employees more than ever during these times. While there should always be a concern for employees, the distinction should be noticed during a time of crisis. More than ever, during a crisis, your employees need to remain emotionally engaged in the task at hand. Giving them a voice during these times is crucial. If they do not have questions and concerns to bring to you, ask. Asking questions will help the leader stay in the loop of what is going on in the field.

During the COVID-19 pandemic, our mayor issued a curfew in our city, mirroring most counties in our state. The curfew was from 10:00 p.m. to 5:00 a.m. daily, and during those hours, we increased the manpower for curfew enforcement. As police officers, we were charged with keeping the piece and enforcing ordinances, such as the curfew in place. There was some concern with some of the officers regarding making contact with people while conducting a traffic stop. Some would comment that they were being put in harm's way by conducting the stops. While it was definitely a dangerous situation, it was the job that we signed up for.

Regardless, we wanted our officers to have a voice, so we brought up their concerns and asked for feedback. Some of the officers suggested that we stop vehicles traveling during the curfew hours but not get too close to the vehicle in case the driver may have been infected by the virus. Some suggested that if we were only enforcing a curfew, we should not even ask for their driver's license so that less contact was made with the driver. Much of the feedback obtained made sense, and we were able to adjust our tactics to keep them safe while performing the required duties. Allowing them to give input and letting them know that their voice matters went a long way with them, which eased up some concerns.

Certainly, during a crisis, there will be a natural fear, uncertainty, or anxiety in employees with what is going on. For those reasons, leaders must demonstrate empathy and put their best foot forward to showcase their care for them getting the job done and an alertness to the needs of the employees. Effectively performing during a crisis may be a moment of truth opportunity for competent and hardworking employees. During incidents of crisis, informal leaders will be identified as a result of their extraordinary performance.

During Hurricane Irma in August 2017, our city endured significant damage from the category 5 storm. We spent several days on the recovery efforts restoring our city and assisting residents. Though my daughter, Abigail, was only three years old at the time and my three young boys were home with only my wife, I did not return home for five days after the storm hit. At that time, I was a sergeant, and there was no way that I could leave the women and men that I supervised during a time like that.

Knowing that I had left my family prepared with all the essential supplies necessary and fortunately having full contact with them via cellular phone, I felt confident that I could stay and complete the task with my employees. On one of the recovery days, there was around eighteen hours straight that we spent inside a trailer park, providing for the residents and trying to restore utilities. I spent most of the day with our mayor, Yoiset De La Cruz, who had also spent several days away from home.

Having our mayor on the frontline with us, dirty and unshaven as we were, gave us a sense of security and motivation to complete the task. I was asked by him at one point to go home and get some rest, but I respectfully disregarded the order and kindly stated that I would be there until the end. We eventually were able to bring some normalcy to the low-income community which brought a sense of accomplishment to me after all our hard work. I was motivated by several things during that crisis. I was first motivated by the ultimate goal. I was also motivated by a great leader on the frontline with us. But I was most motivated by my subordinates who were seeing their leader on the battlefield with them until the end of the mission. Soon after everything went back to normal after Hurricane Irma, I was promoted to the rank of lieutenant by our mayor.

During every recovery effort of a crisis, I have seen politicians arrive at a location only long enough to have their assistant take a few good photographs of them to post on their social media accounts. Or maybe get some camera time with the media then disappear. Then when seen on a social media account or news stations, one would think they have been there all day for the recovery efforts when in fact they really only came by for a publicity cameo. While politics will always be politics, it is sad to see someone take credit that they do not deserve and forget to praise and recognize the ground troops that are actually out there getting their hands dirty.

I stated earlier that we learn from life experiences and supervisors the things to replicate and the things to not replicate professionally and personally. The example was always present to me especially during crises. Our mayor was on the battlefield with us, working alongside his employees while others stopped by to make their cameos then disappear. During the COVID-19 pandemic, I would even get an occasional call or text message from the mayor, showing appreciation for my hard work. Simple little actions that give you fuel for the next day go a long way.

After a Crisis

The type of leader you are has an impact on how you will handle a crisis. Your effectiveness during a noncrisis time will assist you during a time of crisis. Your leadership development journey should prepare you to lead in any situation, even if it is a crisis that you were not prepared for. But crises do not last forever, in the words of Abraham Lincoln, "And this, too, shall pass." Your personnel must be made aware that the new "normal" will end and things will get back to what they used to be.

Many organizations emerge from a crisis stronger and more united than they were before. A leader of an organization must make sure to transition along with employees from crisis mode to normal operations. This can take some time depending on the extent of the crisis endured. The beginning stages of the transition should include a debriefing on all that was done and what can be done differently, given a similar crisis occur. As part of the debriefing, employees must be allowed to give feedback and suggestions before any policies are put into action. When it comes to improving crisis strategies, it is important to pay attention to what the frontline women and men have to say regarding approaches to addressing future crises.

Aligning shared suggestions from all the stakeholders will build a stronger bond within the organization and give everyone a feeling of ownership in the implementations of future planning. With that, an official action plan must be created to guide your organization through a future crisis. Since all organizations are susceptible to crises, it is critical to keep your team members included and engaged with the vision and mission of the organization when implementing future strategies. When given the opportunity to give their input, they will have a feeling of responsibility and sense of accountability in the planning and execution of future crises.

Leadership is a very important role, especially during a time of crisis. While serving employees during a crisis, it is important to remind them that a back-to-normal tomorrow is the goal and that "we will get through it." There is no better time to be effective leaders than during a crisis. Great leaders will make people feel safe and make the organization stronger while addressing the negative impacts of a crisis.

Chapter Thirteen

Second Nature Habits

Have you ever stopped to think about your habits and how they impact your daily life? Habits form when we repeat a behavior that becomes unconsciously automatic after enacted on continuously. Since 90 percent of our everyday behavior is based on habits, we must become the leaders that we want to be by creating the fitting habits to effectively lead. John Dryden said, "We first make our habits, and then our habits make us." Habits thus become second nature actions.

As discussed earlier, employees are weary of change, but leaders must always desire to make modifications to the habits that will hinder their leadership success. For some, changing habits can be difficult, but the ability to adapt to an effective habit is crucial to your second nature leadership success. Since leaders are lifelong learners, incorporating habit adjustments into your leadership self-development is an additional component in your leadership initiative. Habits change into character, and when positive leadership acts become second nature, you will hold the keys to leadership success.

We must work on making our leadership actions our allies instead of enemies. In positively adjusting our daily habits, the actions will become unconscious behavior. On your first day ever driving to a new job, you would need to pay close attention to what street you are on and the route that you are taking. You are conscious of where you are going and surely do not want to be late on your first day because you got lost. But after several times taking the route to work, your mind will automatically take you there without even thinking of the way. Your mind is programmed to take the same path every day, and at times, you may have been so focused on your favorite morning show or podcast that you couldn't believe you were already at work. The route is now programmed in your mind, and you can get there without even thinking about it.

Leadership actions can also be performed instinctively when repeated multiple times. Many leaders have unconsciously created leadership techniques that result in successful outcomes. Others may need to consciously repeat the actions before they become second nature. No matter what competencies you wish to acquire, it takes several repetitive practices in order to acquire it as a skill. Just as the world's top athletes repeated their skills millions of times over in sports, your actions in your leadership expertise must, too, be repeated in order to build consistency at the skill.

Repetition is the main principle of all learning, and the effects of your habits will multiply when you repeat them. If one truly cares about the quality of learning, they must design repetitive engagements into their daily routine. A mindful effort to want to improve your leadership skills must be present before your actions will become second nature. Being positive and productive in our daily lives as a leader will create a comfortable work environment. Continuously conducting yourself in a positive way will become the norm, and you will be seen in that light by employees.

Successful leaders seek to gain the trust of employees and customers. Continuously exerting a positive attitude helps work get performed better. Second nature depends on how much a person acts in a particular way. Your second nature leadership habits will rub off on your work environment and be repeated by others. We know this because we have seen it when people that live together for many years develop similar habits. The habits can be desirable or undesirable depending on who is exerting them dominantly. We can all acquire unnatural qualities; therefore, a leader must be the one exerting positive ones.

Some sought-after qualities are easier to develop than others. God created some of us heavy and others slim, and it would not be impossible for a heavyset person to slim down. Of course, it will not come easy.

For some of us that have a hard time changing certain natural ways, the adjustment may not be easy. Over a period of time with a dedicated mindset, picking up new leadership traits and putting them into action will help you inch toward becoming a better second nature leaders.

There is a big difference between a manager and a leader, of course. A manager is more concerned with their own and the organization's success. A leader empowers the lives of employees and cares about their well-being, motivating them to greatness, which will in turn benefit the organization. Many leaders will admit that they began as a manager and blossomed into a leader. While management is a necessary part of any organization, leadership will take things to the next level.

Managers have habits that keep things organized and have somewhat of an obsessive-compulsive personality for paying attention to functional details. But a manager, too, can adjust their executive habits and turn them into second nature leadership traits. Actually, a manager is in the perfect position to adjust their traits. They already care for the qualities and functions of the organization. Their focus, while continuing on the success of the organization, can turn to a vision of how to inspire their team to go above and beyond.

Some managers have been seen treating customers very differently than their employees. When a manager begins to enhance their people skills toward their team as they do their customers, greater things will happen. A manager that transforms themselves into a leader will soon perform the traits in second nature as they did their management skills. Their ways of telling people what to do will turn their ways into inspiring people to do them.

When transitioning your behaviors and habits from a non-influential manager to a highly effective leader, identification of effective and noneffective actions must be analyzed and adjusted for future occasions. All experiences can be learned from, but the only way to alter actions is to examine experiences and learn from them. The act of giving structure to learning experiences was described in a book by Graham Gibbs called *Learning by Doing*, where Gibbs describes learning from specific situations that he describes as the Gibbs' Reflective Cycle.

Graham Gibbs is a sociologist and psychologist that offered a description of the framework for examining experiences. In his manuscript, Gibbs examined cyclic nature and how it lends itself well to repeated experiences, which allows you to learn from things that either went well or not so well. His model included six stages of reflection which were description, feelings, evaluation, analysis, a conclusion, and an action plan. Many of the stages in this model are already performed by us in many reflecting situations and gives us a way to restructure our thinking in phases.

Reflection is important for learning and developing second nature traits. Once you have identified a habit that needs adjusting, you can now diagnose a remedy for alteration. Since a habit is a way that your brain automatically follows, you will need to reengineer your thought process and execute new actions repeatedly until the actions become second nature. With a small amount of discipline and consistency, you can create second nature habits that will be sure to stick.

Chapter Fourteen

Putting It All Together

The dictionary defines second nature as "a characteristic or habit in someone that appears to be instinctive because that person has behaved in a particular way so often." What that means is that in order for something to become second nature, actions must be repeated several times. Now, with information in each of the chapters in this book, make it a point to perform some of the actions on a daily basis. At the end of each day, ask yourself, "What impact did I make today in the employees and in the organization's growth and development?"

That's it! There is no magic formula and no need to have a bookshelf full of leadership books to figure it out. I'll be the first to admit that I was not a natural-born leader. I was not even a natural-born people person, but through desire and meaningful repetition, I have made my favorable and effective actions second nature. Review the chapters in this book, apply the traits constantly, and make your leadership style also become second nature. Simple actions performed repetitively will boost your leadership qualities and create the results that every leader and follower desires.

The main requirement of leadership success is to have the complete desire to transform your ways in order to lead successfully. As I have stated many times, leaders are made, not born; therefore, like everything else that illustrates progress, a leader has to possess a conscientious passion to alter methods of dealing with leading an organization. As said by John Maxwell, "We cannot become what we need by remaining what we are."

Here is a review:

First in, Last Out. It starts with hard work, and if you are already in a supervisory position, chances are you worked hard to get there. If you are not, then get with it and bust your butt to get recognized. Be a "student of the game," learning everything about your trade and ditch the alarm clock! Let your motivation wake you up in the morning. If you are not yet in a supervisory position, be an informal leader among your coworkers. Very few will be put into a supervisory position without a track record of hard work. Hard work leads to self-improvement. When you work hard, amazing things happen. I promise!

Employees Are Awesome. Take care of your employees, and they will take care of your business.

Remember, they are the "end user," and they need to feel like that truck driver traveling across the country with a valuable message on the back of their trailer. When speaking to employees, be the leader that makes them feel important, not the manager that is trying to sound important. Besides, we are nothing without the personnel that operate the functions of our organization. This function is a leader's secret weapon to obtaining desired productivity and a sense of purpose with the company.

Sometimes Your Coffee Has to Get Cold. Slow down for a minute. Listen and pay attention. When you include "checking the pulse" into your daily routine, you'll be amazed of the benefits that will come out of it. Also, get off your electronic devices and pay attention to what is being said, making eye contact and giving positive feedback, whether you are encountering a customer or interacting with an employee. Listen to understand, not to reply. Building professional relationships and connecting with employees will let them know that you are one of them and that will make them more motivated to work for the organization.

Embrace Change. A computer introduced in the workplace seemed like a UFO to me. It later proved to be one of the most valuable tools in every organizations. Expect that change is inevitable. Embrace them and present them properly to employees. Properly address the saying "That's the way we have always done it." If changes occur in our daily lives, such as fashion and hairstyles, then expect that organizational changes will also constantly occur. Be a change agent for the betterment of the organization and its members. Change affects your most important assets, your people. Clearly, communicating organizational changes while aligning the changes to your business will make the change implementation smoother sailing.

Foster Leadership. Work hard on becoming a leader, and once you succeed at that, the true success comes when you are able to grow others. Begin to recognize potential in your team members early on. Train your personnel so that they are able to perform the functions of the organization in your absence. Train employees well enough so they can leave. Treat them well enough that they don't want to. When you perform a Google search of the word "leadership," over two billion results come up. There is so much information out there on leadership development and very little on fostering leadership. If you are fortunate to be in a leadership position, one of your main duties is now to create more leaders.

Like a Marriage. We spend over one third of our lives at work, and your coworkers become like family. In business and marriage, loyalty, trust, and keeping your word is an essential recipe for a healthy and lasting relationship. A spouse can usually identify when we had a bad day at work. A leader should be able to build a strong enough relationship with employees where they, too, can identify issues affecting them. An organization, like a marriage, should have a "we" mentality and should never be about yourself. Like a marriage, you have to be willing to put the work in to get the gratifying results. Make sure to build a family-like bond and care for them on their good days and be there for them on their bad days.

Motivation. Motivation must be constantly administered. We already know that bathing doesn't last, and that is why it is recommended daily. Accept the fact that not all personnel in your organization will be on board with the vision and mission, and some will be harder to motivate than others. Do not exhaust all your time trying to motivate the small percentage of employees that cannot be motivated and focus primarily on the ones that you can. Utilize the "staircase of motivation" philosophy and try get employees on that next step. Remember that gym memberships are in place because humans run out of motivation and drive. It is a normal human imperfection. Oh yea, and don't forget about motivating yourself.

Problem and Conflict Solving. Be a problem-solving leader. Your value depends on how well your problem and conflict solving skills are. When your boss says "We have a problem!" your reply should be, "Let's find a solution!" When you are able to solve organizational problems, you will bring more worth to yourself as a member of the team. Conflicts will inevitably occur in the workplace and must be addressed immediately. Having the right people on the bus is important, but ignoring conflict can result in toxic employees gradually pulling others off the bus with them. Don't let it happen! Identify issues early and decide a plan of action to address them. Try to understand the root of the problem and create strategies to solve them. Never disregard a problem and hope that it will disappear. You owe it to your members to address them.

Leading Up. Be the leader of leaders. Embrace the idea that one of your key responsibilities as a leader is to make your boss look exceptionally successful. Holding a leadership rank does not necessarily mean that you are required only to lead the personnel under your command. Be persuasive enough so that the boss agrees with your decisions. Run the organization as if you were the owner, pass the credit up, and never make the CEO look bad. Not all leaders want to be led, but when you lighten your boss's load and tactfully come up with solutions that will make her or him shine, you will add additional value to them as well as yourself.

Recognition, Praise, and Appreciation. Never leave recognition, praise, or appreciation out of your leadership engagements. Know that all three are important and a little different from each other. They should always be task specific and not generalized as they will become meaningless. Be detailed when showing appreciation and praising. Offer assistance and occasionally get your hands dirty alongside employees. Never give fake recognition, rather work on motivating the employee up the staircase of motivation so that recognition-worthy events become present. Recognition and praise are essential to an outstanding workplace, and appreciation is a fundamental human need. Properly administering the three will amount to a positive response in the workplace.

Custom Leadership. There is no one-size-fits-all way to lead. Leadership styles will need to be customized depending on employee age groups and tenure with the organization. If you keep in mind that there is nothing specifically "wrong" with a particular generation, you will begin to understand various generations a little better. Keep in mind when asked if leaders are born or made, they are made because of the fact that we have to constantly adjust our leadership styles to the various generations in the workforce. Study your employees, identify what works for each specific generation, and adjust accordingly. Pay attention to your leadership style as well and resist stagnation. Adapt to the times and fit it to the needs of organizational progress.

Leading through Crisis. The formulation of successfully leading during crisis begins long before crisis strikes. When a crisis becomes present, our responsibility as leaders is to support our personnel and clearly communicate goals. A leader must make sure to be present and available to employees and give them a voice, allowing feedback and suggestions for the task at hand.

While there will be a clear focus on the greater goal, the leader must show concern for employees more than ever during these times. The soldiers carrying out the tasks must have a clear vision of the goal. They must feel supported and must be given the resources necessary to complete the job.

Second Nature Habits. Repetition is the main principle of all learning. Quality leadership actions can become instinctive when they are repeated multiple times. The ability to adapt to an effective habit is crucial in creating second nature qualities. Positively adjusting your daily habits will create the unconscious behavior required to successfully lead. In order to succeed at leading, one must incorporate positive leadership habits that will become second nature into their lifelong leadership learnings. Just as your mind can become programmed to take your route from home to work without even thinking about it when continuously traveled, your mind, too, can be programmed to perform quality leadership skills without thinking about it. Work on it and incorporate it into your leadership development.

Furthermore, reflect on your actions and encounters and diagnose a remedy for alteration and apply the results until they become second nature actions.

In Closing

Leadership dedication and the desire to adjust habits is the key to becoming a second nature leader. It is required that you continually chip away at the qualities required to lead well and make adjustments as needed. Consider you want to get your body and health into great shape. Every board-certified doctor that you ask will give you the same solution. Diet and exercise! It sounds pretty simple, but you will need to eat well and workout to get the desired results, right?

When you begin to work out, you will not see drastic results immediately, but with a little discipline and dedication, you will begin to see some results. Missing a day or two at the gym and having a cheat meal on occasion will probably not affect you much, but if you constantly neglect your diet and exercise regimen, your body will surely begin to show it. The same goes for your leadership regimen. If you only perform valuable leadership qualities once in a while, you probably will not see much of a result but if you constantly practice effective leadership qualities, then they will eventually become second nature, and you will be sure to see great results.

Leadership is a journey with no completion date or final targeted number to reach. Most organizations create deadlines and goals for the employees to meet, which gives them closure on a specific task until the next assignment begins. Employees may have a goal of hitting the highest number of sales or do better than a competitor, but a leader has no final end in sight for their goal. Leadership requires constant second nature leadership actions to get employees to feel and perform a certain way, then maintenance of your progress is constantly required for employees to remain at desired performance levels.

Reading this manuscript alone will not fully enhance your leadership skills. It will not even improve your supervisory skills or even the way you interact with employees. Your leadership development will only increase when you continuously apply the leadership tactics that I have described and make habit adjustments to ineffective actions. This book has not casted a leadership spell on you that has made you a better leader, rather given you some tools of the trade that you must passionately use on a daily basis until they become second nature.

The focus of this book has been in part about the importance of work hard, how to make employees feel awesome, motivating and appreciating employees, embracing and creating change, creating more leaders, solving problems and conflicts, recognizing performance, customizing your leadership, and leading through crisis. In all those leadership tasks, the tables ultimately need to be turned on you and what actions you will take to carry them out. The actions of leadership profiled in this book can take your leadership success to the next level. But this can only be done by you as a leader and the qualities that will come as a result of repetitive actions. Specifically, you need to know where you want to go as a leader and draw out a road map on how to get there. Focus on what you need to be doing in your life and do it. Seek to exemplify the virtues of second nature habits in your life and begin to execute them.

The only way that your leadership skills will be sharpened and become second nature is when they are constantly performed. Eventually, you will not have to ask yourself at the end of the day what difference you may have made. The skills will be performed without thinking, and you will join the elite team of second nature leaders.

Good luck and enjoy the process!

About the Author

Freddy Caceres is an executive police administrator that oversees the operations of a police department in the Miami, Florida, area. He has over twenty years of management and leadership experience and has studied several qualities and shortcomings of leaders for this manuscript as well as for his own leadership success. He has worked as a patrol sergeant, detective bureau supervisor, and operations lieutenant within the agency. He started his leadership journey in the early '90s at a large telecommunications company where he worked his way up the corporate ladder as an operations manager to eventually be responsible for over four hundred employees throughout his tenure with the company.

Freddy has worked as an adjunct criminal justice college professor and has been a guest speaker at colleges and high schools to present leadership in criminal justice lectures. Throughout his law enforcement career, Freddy has attended several criminal justice, management, and leadership related courses. He is a graduate of the Southern Police Institute's Command Officer Development Course and holds a bachelor's degree in criminal justice management and a master's degree in executive management. After obtaining his master's degree, Freddy put school on hold to concentrate on his position as a lieutenant, but during the completion of this book, he was actively working on his PhD in criminal justice leadership. He is married to the love of his life, Lina, and has four children, Ethan, Wesley, Ryan, and Abigail.

CPSIA information can be obtained
at www.ICGtesting.com
Printed in the USA
LVHW081929261120
672780LV00034B/308